Ruby's Story

A Drama in Two Acts

by Ron Osborne

A SAMUEL FRENCH ACTING EDITION

FOUNDED 1830
NEW YORK HOLLYWOOD LONDON TORONTO
SAMUELFRENCH.COM

Copyright © 2004, 2009 by Ron Osborne

ALL RIGHTS RESERVED

CAUTION: Professionals and amateurs are hereby warned that *RUBY'S STORY* is subject to a Licensing Fee. It is fully protected under the copyright laws of the United States of America, the British Commonwealth, including Canada, and all other countries of the Copyright Union. All rights, including professional, amateur, motion picture, recitation, lecturing, public reading, radio broadcasting, television and the rights of translation into foreign languages are strictly reserved. In its present form the play is dedicated to the reading public only.

The amateur live stage performance rights to *RUBY'S STORY* are controlled exclusively by Samuel French, Inc., and licensing arrangements and performance licenses must be secured well in advance of presentation. PLEASE NOTE that amateur Licensing Fees are set upon application in accordance with your producing circumstances. When applying for a licensing quotation and a performance license please give us the number of performances intended, dates of production, your seating capacity and admission fee. Licensing Fees are payable one week before the opening performance of the play to Samuel French, Inc., at 45 W. 25th Street, New York, NY 10010.

Licensing Fee of the required amount must be paid whether the play is presented for charity or gain and whether or not admission is charged.

Stock licensing fees quoted upon application to Samuel French, Inc.

For all other rights than those stipulated above, apply to: Samuel French, Inc., 45 W. 25th Street, New York, NY 10010.

Particular emphasis is laid on the question of amateur or professional readings, permission and terms for which must be secured in writing from Samuel French, Inc.

Copying from this book in whole or in part is strictly forbidden by law, and the right of performance is not transferable.

Whenever the play is produced the following notice must appear on all programs, printing and advertising for the play: "Produced by special arrangement with Samuel French, Inc."

Due authorship credit must be given on all programs, printing and advertising for the play.

ISBN 978-0-573-69692-3   Printed in U.S.A.   #29107

No one shall commit or authorize any act or omission by which the copyright of, or the right to copyright, this play may be impaired.

No one shall make any changes in this play for the purpose of production.

Publication of this play does not imply availability for performance. Both amateurs and professionals considering a production are strongly advised in their own interests to apply to Samuel French, Inc., for written permission before starting rehearsals, advertising, or booking a theatre.

No part of this book may be reproduced, stored in a retrieval system, or transmitted in any form, by any means, now known or yet to be invented, including mechanical, electronic, photocopying, recording, videotaping, or otherwise, without the prior written permission of the publisher.

IMPORTANT BILLING AND CREDIT REQUIREMENTS

All producers of *RUBY'S STORY* must give credit to the Author of the Play in all programs distributed in connection with performances of the Play, and in all instances in which the title of the Play appears for the purposes of advertising, publicizing or otherwise exploiting the Play and/or a production. The name of the Author *must* appear on a separate line on which no other name appears, immediately following the title and *must* appear in size of type not less than fifty percent of the size of the title type.

RUBY'S STORY was produced by 13th Street Repertory Company in New York City (Edith O'Hara, Artistic Director) May 20 through July 10, 2004. It was directed by Troy Miller and the cast included Kelly Barrett, Hella Bel, Edward Bergtold, Amy Bizjak, Catherine Hennessey, James Nocito, Mary Anne Sayre and Elizabeth Ulmer.

RUBY'S STORY returned to 13th Street Repertory Theatre in New York City (Edith O'Hara, Artistic Director; Sandra Nordgren, General Manager and Associate Artistic Director) on June 12, 2009. The production was directed by Niles Mott; the stage manager was Anna Grijalva. The cast was as follows:

ADULT RUBY .... Kathryn Neville Browne
YOUNG RUBY............................... Gina Marie Jamieson
HELGA .... Ruthellen Cheney
ROSE.. Eloise Ayala
FRIEDA .... Jessica Rhodes
WALTER... Mike Pirozzi
GRACE.. Julie Hays
SID/STAN .... Jonathan Harper Schlieman

RUBY'S STORY was recognized in a dozen national playwriting competitions and developed through readings in Los Angeles (The Road Theatre Company), Jersey City (The Attic Theatre), St. Louis (First Run Theatre), Abingdon, VA (Barter Theatre) and Chicago (Chicago Dramatists).

CHARACTERS

ADULT RUBY – early 60s
YOUNG RUBY – a young 16
HELGA – her sister, 21
ROSE – her sister, 24
FRIEDA – her sister, almost 20
WALTER –their father, early-50s
GRACE – their mother, early-50s
SID – Frieda's friend, 24*
STAN – Rose's fiancé, mid-20s*

*Consideration should be given to having the same actor portray both roles (note: both characters face similar challenges during the play). Also, the script calls for Adult Ruby to enter and exits at specific points. Some directors have chosen to keep the character on stage throughout the play (although in the background when not directly involved in the action.) When used in this way, Adult Ruby would seem to float from scene to scene, acting much as a witness to the family's struggles.

TIME

June 1944 (shortly before and immediately following D-Day).

PLACE

The majority of the action takes place in the parlor and on the front steps of Walter and Grace's home located in one of the few fertile valleys just outside Bluefield, West Virginia. Short scenes take place at a dance hall, a farmers' market, Walter's apple orchard, a railroad platform, and a Polish national lodge; these brief sequences should be evocative, created entirely by lighting and sound.

SET

The parlor features simple furniture, dating from the 1930s and earlier (several chairs, a sofa, a floor lamp, tables, etc.). A console radio occupies a prominent position in the room. There are two doors, one that leads to the balance of the house (unseen) and a second that exits to a front porch and steps (both – as well as a small portion of the home's front lawn – should be seen) Lighting should allow each of these areas to be lit independently. There should be nothing fancy about any aspects of the home or the attire worn by the characters—these are simple people who live a simple existence in challenging times. Also, it is hoped that scenes (the only definitive break occurs between acts) flow seamlessly, assisted by lighting, sound effects, music, etc.

HISTORICAL PERSPECTIVE

In the late 1800s, the world's largest deposit of bituminous coal was discovered under the hills of Pocahontas, VA. As a result, nearby Bluefield, WV grew overnight from a sleepy little town to a booming metropolis. Before long, the city boasted a population of 25,000 and was known throughout the Appalachians as "Little New York." Adolph Hitler – aware of Bluefield's importance to the U.S. war effort – put the town on the list of targets for German air raids. As a result, air practice drills – "blackouts" as they were called – were common in the area throughout the war.

As one might imagine, Bluefield's coal rush attracted immigrants from many countries, including thousands of Poles who established a national lodge and other reminders of home in the city. As is true today, relations between the existing population – primarily German and Scotch-Irish – and the more recent immigrants weren't always cordial.

ARTISTIC STATEMENT

Although set in 1944, *Ruby's Story* addresses a number of important issues we face today; namely, the devastating cost of war – not just on the battlefield – but on the home front as well. Discussed, too, are the ramifications of ethic and religious intolerance, not unlike that suffered by more recent immigrant and migrant groups.

*Dedicated with love to my parents, Edna and Joe,
whose lives are reflected in the story Ruby tells.*

ACT ONE

(The stage is empty. Lights – dim rather than bright – come up on a parlor of an old house. After a moment, **ADULT RUBY** *enters. Dressed in a dark dress, she strolls through the room. We sense she's been here before and the things that surround her have special meaning. After a moment, she steps to an old photo album, picks it up, opens it. At that moment, lights come up full – it is as if a warm sun has filled the room. At the same moment, music from the 1930s or early 40s plays on the radio in the parlor.)*

(Abruptly, **YOUNG RUBY** *rushes into the room, chased by* **FRIEDA***. The two circle the space several times, giggling and laughing as they play. Seconds later,* **HELGA** *and* **ROSE** *run up the front steps and into the parlor.* **HELGA** *takes* **ROSE***'s hand, and the two dance to the music. After a moment,* **GRACE** *enters. She watches her daughters as* **WALTER** *– fresh from his orchard – enters from the porch.* **GRACE** *takes his hand, and – although* **WALTER** *is initially reluctant – they also dance. As lights slowly dim to black,* **ROSE** *blows a kiss to* **WALTER***, and the music is down and out. The overall effect borders on the surreal.)*

(After a moment, lights – again dim – come up, shrouding the parlor and **ADULT RUBY** *in a cloud-like darkness not unlike her own clouded recollection of past events in the home. After a moment, she crosses to the porch, looks back into the now empty parlor, then turns and addresses the audience.)*

ADULT RUBY. Our home…"six miles from Bluefield as the crow flies." Pop must've said that a thousand times. Out back, vegetable patches and a fruit orchard, which

— thanks to his hard work — put more than turnips and apples on our table. In front — set in the prettiest little valley you could imagine, surrounded by mountains that rise to the sky — a yard...broad, pretty...the kind of yard I always thought deserved a bigger house. Which would've been nice, considering I shared a tiny bathroom with three older sisters who truly believed cleanliness was next to godliness. You can deal with three sisters and one tub, you can deal with anything. And we did...until the summer of 1944...when it was if there had been a before and an after. That awful feeling...that what we had before that summer began — simple pleasures shared by a family that loved one another — were an illusion. And haunting me still, the uncertainty of it all...What was real?...What wasn't?... To so profoundly change our lives.

(Lights begin to come up some on the parlor. A blue star service flag now hangs from a window, and the characters we saw earlier appear motionless in formal tableau. **WALTER** *sits in a chair adjacent to a radio;* **HELGA** *sits at a writing desk;* **ROSE** *stands in front of a window; and* **YOUNG RUBY** *lies on her back in the center of the group, a magazine in hand. As* **ADULT RUBY** *introduces each character, that character springs into motion or enters. When the introductions are concluded, all characters are going about their business.)*

RADIO ANNOUNCER. "To a chorus of church bells, Allied Forces entered Rome today. From the Little Whitehouse in Warm Springs, Georgia, President Roosevelt told the nation, "The first of the Axis capitals is now in our hands..."

ADULT RUBY. *(The radio is down as she speaks.)* There was Pop of course.

WALTER. Where's my Epsom salt, Grace?

(begins removing his shoes and socks, speaking to himself)

I ask her to bring me my Epsom salt...

ADULT RUBY. He was sure Mama had been put on this earth to serve him. The way she'd cater to him, maybe she was.

(**GRACE** *enters. She crosses to* **WALTER**, *taking care to avoid spilling water from the pan she carries.*)

GRACE. Water does not heat itself, Walter, because you scream, "Bring me my Epsom salt."

(**GRACE** *places the pan in front of* **WALTER** *whose shoes and socks are now off. He puts one foot in the pan, then quickly removes it.*)

WALTER. I'm not a lobster, Grace!

GRACE. Too hot again? Tsk.

RADIO ANNOUNCER. "In the British Isles, the Allied buildup continues..."

WALTER. *(interested in the report on the radio)* Shhh...

RADIO ANNOUNCER. "...Reports indicate more than two million American, Empire and troops of Occupied Nations have massed for a possible invasion of the Continent. The War Department refuses to speculate..."

ADULT RUBY. War was raging around the world. But that summer we had a special focus...England. That's where my sister Helga's husband, Jimmy, was...in the army and...somewhere over there.

(**ADULT RUBY** *turns, looks at* **HELGA** *who leans forward, begins writing.*)

She kept herself busy writing letters – Helga did. That is, when she wasn't helping Pop in his orchard, which was as hardly at all. Some days she'd manage two letters, a feat that amazed me. But I guess when you're in love...

HELGA. Pop, you know all this war stuff gives me the willies.

GRACE. Walter, you know those reports bother Helga. Could we listen to some music please?

(to **HELGA***)*

Would you like to listen to music, sweetie?

(**GRACE** *hesitates, waiting for* **WALTER**'s *approval. He grunts something and* **HELGA** *turns the radio to another station. Big band music is up then under.*)

ADULT RUBY. Helga wasn't the only one who hated the war. My sister Rose hated it too.

(**RUBY** *turns toward* **ROSE**; **ROSE** *folds her arms across her chest.*)

Her Stan – the love of her life – was in the service too. And like Helga's Jimmy – a very long way from home.

(**ADULT RUBY** *turns to* **YOUNG RUBY** *who rises to a sitting position.*)

Then there was me. Barely sixteen when that summer began…a little older, but years wiser when it ended.

GRACE. Isn't that the prettiest music, Rose? Now, who'll dance with me?

(*surveying the possibilities*)

Rose, you love to dance. Dance with me.

ROSE. I don't feel like dancing.

GRACE. (*looking to* **WALTER** *who now has both feet in the pan*) Well, *he* won't dance anymore! Even with his Sunday-go-to-church shoes on and Fred Murray telling him where to put his two left feet…you won't dance with me, will you, Walter? That means…

(*takes* **ROSE**'s *hand*)

ROSE. Mama!

(*reluctantly dances a few revolutions, then pulls away*)

Mama, I told you I don't feel like dancing!

GRACE. (*now waltzing a step or two by herself*) There was a time! Tell her, Walter…the two of us…from one end of the farmers' club to the other … into the wee, wee hours of the morning.

(*stops dancing, whispering to* **ROSE**)

He'd take me home, Rose – kiss me on the cheek. I'd hurry inside, slip off my dancing shoes, put *my* black and blue toes – guess where, Walter? *Into my own pail of Epsom salt.*

YOUNG RUBY. That's funny, Mama.

GRACE. Tell my toes that.

HELGA. Jimmy's a wonderful dancer!

GRACE. *(looking somewhat critically at* **WALTER**, *smiling)* Some people get lucky, sweetie.

HELGA. Except he doesn't like people watching us dance. So we watch everybody else. Makes them nervous... especially Rose and Stan.

GRACE. Now that boy can dance.

ROSE. She made fun of him.

HELGA. That's not true, Rose.

ROSE. *(perhaps acting out her words)* Stan would lift me...whirl me...make me feel like Ginger Rogers. Oh, Stan...!

(abruptly back to reality, looking at **HELGA***)*

And she would whisper!

HELGA. That's not true, Mama!

ROSE. *YOU WHISPERED!*

GRACE. No wonder nobody in his house feels like dancing anymore.

ADULT RUBY. Mama was wrong about that ...

*(***FRIEDA*** explodes into the room, leaving no doubt she has a zest for dancing and for life.* **ADULT RUBY** *turns to her.)*

There was my other sister, Frieda...

FRIEDA. *(with a sense of urgency, motioning to* **YOUNG RUBY***)* Ruby, I need you...

WALTER. What did I tell you, Grace?

GRACE. Acknowledge your father please.

FRIEDA. Pop.

WALTER. Ignores me completely.

FRIEDA. Sorry, Pop.

GRACE. Honey, all your daddy wants –

WALTER. Turn off the music.

GRACE. We're enjoying the music, Walter.

WALTER. *Turn off the music!*
ROSE. *Mama, don't do it!*
GRACE. It's okay, Rose. It's okay.

(**GRACE** *steps quickly to the radio, turning it off. As she does,* **FRIEDA** *crosses to* **YOUNG RUBY***, takes her hand and drags her to feet. An upset* **ROSE** *crosses her arms across her chest.*)

ADULT RUBY. Six days a week, Frieda escaped to nearby Bluefield. There – working in a small factory – she made military uniforms and new friends. And bless her heart, she shared every exciting introduction with me.

(*Hand in hand,* **FRIEDA** *and* **YOUNG RUBY** *exit to the steps of the porch as the parlor lights – as well as those on* **ADULT RUBY** *– begin to dim slowly to black,*)

WALTER. Respect. Is that too much, Grace?
GRACE. Oh, Walter.

(*Lights now down full on parlor and up on the porch steps.* **FRIEDA** *sits on a step as* **RUBY** *circles excitedly in front of her.*)

YOUNG RUBY. What? *What?*
FRIEDA. Guess who I met today.
YOUNG RUBY. Tell me!
FRIEDA. You've got to guess, Ruby!
YOUNG RUBY. Then let's see…maybe you met…
FRIEDA. *Guess!*
YOUNG RUBY. *Franklin Delano Roosevelt!*
FRIEDA. God! Why do I bother with you?
YOUNG RUBY. A boy! You met a boy!
FRIEDA. Actually…I met a man…
YOUNG RUBY. *Tell me…!*
FRIEDA. Well, he's…tall –
YOUNG RUBY. How tall?
 (*holding her hand out in front of her*)
 This tall?

FRIEDA. Lots taller! And he's got gorgeous dark hair. And he's handsome like…like Clark Gable, in person!

YOUNG RUBY. Clark Gable. Ohh!

FRIEDA. When Sidney – Sid. That's what he asked me to call him. When he smiled at me the first time, my heart went –

YOUNG RUBY.	**FRIEDA.**
Pound, pound, pound…	Pound, pound, pound…

FRIEDA. Mr. Lazansky – that's his daddy – he owns the factory – the whole thing. And guess what?

YOUNG RUBY. What?

FRIEDA. I'm going to marry him.

YOUNG RUBY. You're going to marry Mr. Lazansky?

FRIEDA. God, you're stupid, Ruby. I'm marrying Sid.

YOUNG RUBY. You are so full of it, Frieda.

FRIEDA. Well, I am. I just haven't told him yet –

(**GRACE** *appears at the door for a second.*)

GRACE. Supper, girls.

FRIEDA. Don't breathe a word – promise?

YOUNG RUBY. Promise you'll tell me everything.

FRIEDA. We'll see, won't we?

YOUNG RUBY. *Everything!*

FRIEDA. *All right!*

(**FRIEDA** *and* **YOUNG RUBY** *stand and step to the front door which* **RUBY** *holds open for her sister.*)

YOUNG RUBY. Then…after you…

(*motions for* **FRIEDA** *to enter in front of her*)

The soon-to-be…Mrs. Sidney Lazansky…

(**YOUNG RUBY** *and* **FRIEDA** *enter the parlor. Lights are down.*)

(*It is later that evening. The characters have reassembled in the parlor, occupying pretty much the same positions as earlier. A floor lamp helps illuminate the setting, giving the room a deceptively warm glow. The radio is up briefly – perhaps an announcer's voice is heard – then down as* **ADULT RUBY** *addresses the audience.)*

ADULT RUBY. After supper Pop insisted we assemble in the parlor where we'd listen to the radio. At least I'd listen, because I was determined to be the next Louella Parsons or Edward R. Murrow, and I needed all the help I could get.

YOUNG RUBY. *(sits up, attempting to imitate Edward R. Murrow)* This...is London ...

HELGA. *Ruby!*

*(***YOUNG RUBY*** gives* **HELGA** *a dirty look, then assumes her original position; perhaps an old radio commercial is up, then down.)*

ADULT RUBY. Between commercials for Lucky Strike cigarettes and "Wild Root Cream Oil, Chaaarrlie," Mama would regale us with stories, some of which may have even been true. All the while, we'd keep our eyes on Pop, expecting him to fall asleep. Which he did, at eight p.m. sharp.

GRACE. You're going to the farmers' market tomorrow, Walter?

WALTER. *(nearly asleep)* Huh?

GRACE. I said, are you taking produce to Bluefield in the morning?

*(***WALTER*** manages to grunt something after which his head falls forward; he's fully asleep now.)*

ROSE. *(looking at* **WALTER***, sarcastically)* It must be eight o'clock.

*(***GRACE*** rises, steps to the radio, turns it off.)*

HELGA. Thank you, Mama.

GRACE. Something's wrong with me, I guess. Because I loved going to the market with my Papa! Except, of course, that first time.

HELGA. What happened?

GRACE. Well, back then – instead of a truck – we had a wagon. And Mike.

HELGA. Mike was a mule, right?

GRACE. Not just a mule, Helga! The smartest four-legged creature God ever made! So smart Papa would load his baskets at the market, hop on the wagon, say, "Take me home, Mike." Then fall asleep.

ROSE. Another one of her stories.

GRACE. Story, baloney, Rose. There's Papa...sitting on his wagon...his eyes shut...dreaming of radishes or something. Out front, old Mike is clip-clopping along. Where? I had no idea – over a cliff maybe. To make a long *true* story short, *Rose*, Mike pulls up in front of feeding trough in the middle of who-knows where. In a wink, Papa is awake, screaming at the animal to take us home. Which, of course, Mike isn't gonna do...not when his head is buried in a pile of oats..

(laughing)

I believe that's when Papa stopped dreaming of radishes, started dreaming of owning a truck.

(pause, looking at **WALTER** *as she speaks)*

Maybe, Ruby – you would go with him in the morning?

YOUNG RUBY. Mama...

GRACE. I'll go myself. Have the time of my life.

HELGA. Mama asked you a favor, Ruby.

YOUNG RUBY. What are you doing, Helga? Other than writing stupid letters morning and night?

HELGA. Tell her to mind her own business, Mama.

ROSE. Well, I'm not going!

HELGA. Nobody asked you to go, Rose.

YOUNG RUBY. Why can't Rose go, Mama? She doesn't have a job. She never lifts a finger around here –

ROSE. *Stay out of it, Ruby!*

YOUNG RUBY. Why does somebody have to go with him anyway?

ROSE. She's worried he'll have a heart attack – that's why!

GRACE. *(to* **YOUNG RUBY**) He gets pains sometimes in his chest.

ROSE. I told you, Mama...he's too mean to die.

GRACE. I won't listen to that, Rose!

ROSE. Well, he is! And you know it!

(A brief silence. **GRACE** *looks at* **WALTER** *who remains asleep.)*

GRACE. *(softly, to herself)* It's the war I think.

HELGA. What did you say, Mama?

GRACE. I said the war's making him this way.

ROSE. He's afraid we'll win!

GRACE. Oh, Rose!

ROSE. The way he'd argue with Stan...remember, Mama? Mr. Jennings heard him...called him a Nazi –

GRACE. Shhh ...

ROSE. Hates Jews, he said. I know he hates Poles. Hates everybody the Nazi's hate.

GRACE. Tom Jennings doesn't know what he's talking about.

ROSE. Nobody wants to buy his stuff at the market anymore. Does that tell you something?

(beat, looking at **WALTER**)

Oh, I can see him now...bubbling over about Adolph Hitler, of all the crazy, stupid names.

GRACE. All the farmers liked Hitler. All the German farmers.

ROSE. Pop wasn't raised in Germany. He was raised in this house.

GRACE. And confirmed in German. His parents spoke German –

ROSE. He thinks he's German through and through.

FRIEDA. Quick. Wake him up. Tell him it's the wrong time to be German anything.

ROSE. That's what Stan did.
GRACE. I've heard that story too many times, Rose.
HELGA. We've all heard that story too many times.
FRIEDA. Excuse me, Mama…the crickets will be more entertaining.

(She crosses to the front door and exits.)

ROSE. Nobody was drafting Stan –
HELGA. So he enlisted in the Polish Army –
ROSE. Get it right, Helga! The Polish Free Forces!
HELGA. Because Pop was German. We know the story, Rose.
GRACE. Your daddy didn't make Stan do anything, Rose!
ROSE. Think what you want…*all of you!*

*(**GRACE** approaches **ROSE**, attempts to comfort her; **ROSE** resists. Lights slowly dim on the parlor. In the darkness, we hear the sounds of big band music as it might be played in a dance hall. When the lights return, it is the previous August. We see **ROSE** sitting alone, her eyes following dancers we can not see. After a moment, **STAN** appears; he approaches her. He is handsome with a bit of a swagger; in contrast to the previous beat, we see a happier, more approachable **ROSE**.)*

STAN. *(to **ROSE**)* Hello.
ROSE. Hello.
STAN. You do not dance?
ROSE. *(The music is loud, but it's **STAN**'s Polish accent that confuses her.)* I'm sorry. I didn't understand…
STAN. I said…do you not dance?
ROSE. I dance, but…
(hesitates)
STAN. …Yes?
ROSE. Do I know you?
STAN. Ah. Now I understand…
*(tries again, bowing to **ROSE**)*
Hello. My name is Stan. Your name is please…?

ROSE. My name is Rose, but...

(hesitating again)

STAN. Yes...?

(The music that has been playing has concluded.)

ROSE. You're not from around here, are you?

STAN. I am not from around here. You are right.

ROSE. So...then you're from...where?

STAN. *(proudly)* Bluefield, West Virginia, U.S.A.

ROSE. I mean, where are – you know *from*...?

STAN. Where was I born? That is your question –

ROSE. You have an accent, so I figured –

STAN. *(once again, proudly)* I am from Poland.

(The music begins again. It is a slower piece, also from the 40s.)

Will you dance with me, Rose?

ROSE. *(flustered, looking around, wondering if anybody's watching)* Oh, I don't think so – not now – I'm sorry.

STAN. You do not like the music?

ROSE. Oh, the music's nice. I...just...well...I...

STAN. I am sorry – it is me. I should not have –

ROSE. No, no. You're very nice. I mean you *seem* to be very nice...

STAN. Then honor me, Rose. Dance with me please...

*(**STAN** takes **ROSE**'s hand. She's remains hesitant.)*

Dance with me, Rose...

*(**STAN** pulls **ROSE** to a standing position. They look at one another for a moment, then dance...first awkwardly, then as if they belonged together. As **STAN** and **ROSE** dance, lights dim on them and come up on **ADULT RUBY**.)*

ADULT RUBY. The Stanislaw Kulikowski Rose danced with that evening in August 1943 – and who courted her for the next five months – had come to West Virginia, as had so many others – to work in the mines. That he was Polish won him no points with Pop who – almost overnight it seemed – had become the living, breathing reincarnation of Kaiser Wilhelm. That made for stimulating conversation, and introduced me to international diplomacy, or the lack of it...*especially* after Stan proposed and Rose accepted.

(Lights now return to the parlor where **GRACE**, **HELGA**, **YOUNG RUBY**, *and* **ROSE** *occupy the positions they had just moments before. After a moment,* **FRIEDA** *re-enters.)*

FRIEDA. Air raid drill, Mama.

GRACE. Not another black-out?

ADULT RUBY. Three weeks before the wedding, Stan announced he was leaving the Pocahontas Mining Company and Rose, to join the Polish Free Forces in England. Rose was devastated – completely and utterly – and claimed Pop was responsible.

FRIEDA. Mr. Schmidt said cover the windows till nine o'clock.

ADULT RUBY. From then on...nothing was the same.

GRACE. Board them up till this awful war's over – that's what I say.

(Lights down on **ADULT RUBY**, *as* **GRACE** *lowers a shade, turns off the lamp. The parlor is now dimly lit; there's a moment of silence.)*

YOUNG RUBY. Hard to write letters now, isn't it, Helga?

HELGA. Shut up, Ruby!

YOUNG RUBY. *(after a moment, again doing her best to imitate Edward R. Murrow)* Tonight I saw the lights go out –

HELGA. Good God, Ruby!

GRACE. Let her practice, sweetie.

YOUNG RUBY. And with it came the awful realization that war may not be as distant as we had thought –

HELGA. Make her stop, Mama!

YOUNG RUBY. That it could rage here...among us...in America.

HELGA. She thinks she's funny, Mama!

ROSE. She thinks she's Edward R. Murrow, *again.*

YOUNG RUBY. You think so…really?

ROSE.	**HELGA.**
No!	*No!*

YOUNG RUBY. I'll change my name, of course. I don't think anybody in New York City is going to like the sound of "The News With Ruby Zweifel."

HELGA. Be quiet, Ruby!

YOUNG RUBY. Rebecca Ruby. Whatdaya think, Helga? "From New York City, the Columbia Broadcasting System brings you "The News with Rebecca Ruby. Brought to you by

(imitating the radio commercial, having fun doing it)

Bromo-Seltzer-Bromo-Selzer-Bromo –

ROSE. *Stop it!*

(another short silence)

YOUNG RUBY. It's okay, Mama. I'll go with Pop in the morning.

GRACE. Thank you, Ruby. Help him with the trays please. The heavy ones. They're the ones I worry about.

(another short silence)

HELGA. I wonder what they're doing?

GRACE. Jimmy and Stan, huh?

HELGA. I wonder if they're scared.

ROSE. Of course they're scared, aren't you?

FRIEDA. I've heard they're having a wonderful time.

HELGA. Who's having a wonderful time?

FRIEDA. Our boys.

ROSE. Where did you hear something crazy like that?

HELGA. You say the stupidest things, Frieda.

FRIEDA. It was on the radio, Helga! The pretty English girls like our boys…our boys *really* like the pretty English girls – !

GRACE. Frieda!

FRIEDA. I've also heard –

ROSE. **HELGA.**
Frieda, shut up!   *Frieda, shut up!*

(another brief silence)

HELGA. Jimmy's birthday. It's tomorrow, Mama.

GRACE. June the sixth. And, so far from home. Tsk.

FRIEDA. Everybody, wish Jimmy a happy birthday

HELGA. That's bad luck, Frieda!

FRIEDA. Talk about stupid, Helga.

HELGA. To wish somebody "Happy Birthday" *before* their birthday – it's *bad luck!*

FRIEDA. Everybody together now…

HELGA. No – !

GRACE. Frieda –

FRIEDA. *(singing, taunting* **HELGA** *as she does) Happy birthday, Jimmy…happy birthday, Jimmy…HAPPY BIRTHDAY –*

HELGA. *Stop it!*

*(****FRIEDA*** *stops but not before* ***HELGA*** *has begun to weep. As* ***GRACE*** *comforts her, lights dim to black. Lights now up on* ***ADULT RUBY****.)*

ADULT RUBY. The next morning – Tuesday, June the 6th, 1944…Jimmy's twenty-second birthday as it turned out – Pop and I loaded up his old Dodge truck and headed to the small produce market in downtown Bluefield. I don't remember much about coming or going, but what happened there, I'll never forget. It began innocently enough…Pop talking to a couple of older men…farmers from around here I remember thinking. Seconds later they were yelling at him. At first, I couldn't make out what they were shouting. Then I understood….

VOICES. *(Offstage) Hitler lover…*GODDAMN NAZI…*NAZI…*

(Lights down on ***ADULT RUBY*** *and up on* ***YOUNG RUBY*** *and* ***WALTER****; they're at a market; lighting alone creates the illusion.)*

YOUNG RUBY. Everything's unloaded, Pop.

(**WALTER** *is breathing deeply, and* **YOUNG RUBY** *is anxious to leave.*)

Pop, did you hear me say I got everything?

WALTER. Can't an old man catch his breath?

YOUNG RUBY. I'll wait in the truck. Okay?

WALTER. What they said to me, Ruby –

YOUNG RUBY. I wasn't listening, Pop.

WALTER. The names they called me…they're not true.

YOUNG RUBY. Why didn't you tell them that? When they were yelling at you, Pop, why didn't you tell them they were wrong?

WALTER. We need to get home.

YOUNG RUBY. Pop, you should've told them.

(**WALTER** *steps out of view.* **YOUNG RUBY** *eyes follow him as the lights go down on her.*)

(*Lights up on* **GRACE** *and* **HELGA** *who sit in the parlor. It is a short time later.* **GRACE** *is busily shelling peas.*)

GRACE. You could help.

HELGA. I don't like peas, Mama.

GRACE. Well, I'm not crazy about them either. Probably because I'm the one who has to shell them.

HELGA. Rose helps some.

GRACE. Rose is slow. She spills more than she gets in the bowl. Which means I shell most of them…then get to sweep up the rest. So…
(*smiling at* **HELGA**)
I just do it myself, like everything else around here.

HELGA. Maybe if you'd let us help –

GRACE. I love you to death, sweetie. But all you know how to do is fry an egg. And I've learned…Rose can't be trusted with a dish in this house.

HELGA. The Thanksgiving turkey! Oh, Mama, you cried –

GRACE. Not because the fool thing ended up staring at me cavity side up in the middle of my kitchen floor. I cried because my mama's stuffing recipe didn't call for slivers of my favorite blue and white platter.

HELGA. Rose dropped it on purpose.

GRACE. Shame on you!

HELGA. Where was the platter from, Mama?

GRACE. You know where it was from. Pop's family brought it from…Germany.

(GRACE considers the reality of HELGA's claim.)

If it'd been empty, maybe. But a twenty-two pound turkey. I don't –

HELGA. Think what you want. Spoil us, too, if that's what you want.

GRACE. I've have so few things I value. If I spoil all of you to protect what I have, so be it.

HELGA. That's what I want to do…spoil Jimmy rotten. Oh, I'll feed that boy morning, noon and night –

GRACE. I hope he likes eggs sunny side up.

HELGA. Give him the best-looking sons anybody ever had. Oh, I never cared about another boy.

GRACE. He was the only boy you ever went out with.

HELGA. He was the *one*, Mama! *I knew it!*

GRACE. That cute Dietrich boy. He thought the sun rose and set on you. You didn't give him a look.

HELGA. Jerome Dietrich was nine years old.

GRACE. Well, he grew up.

HELGA. Yes, he did! He's fourteen now, and I'm twenty-one.

GRACE. I'm trying to make you smile, sweetie.

HELGA. How can I smile, Mama? It's Jimmy's birthday. I'm scared!

(ROSE enters. She sees GRACE shelling peas.)

ROSE. Need help, Mama?

GRACE. Shelling peas? Oh, I don't think so, Rose.

ROSE. *(to* **HELGA***, upon seeing* **HELGA** *wipe a tear from her eye)* What's wrong with her?

GRACE. I wouldn't let her help either.

HELGA. If I want to cry, Rose –

ROSE. Jimmy again, huh?

HELGA. He *is* my husband!

ROSE. Stan and I aren't married – that makes a difference –

GRACE. Don't start with that, Rose.

ROSE. That's what she's saying, Mama!

HELGA. You and your crazy imagination.

ROSE. You think I don't know what everybody's saying… Stan didn't want to marry me, so he used the war as an excuse?

GRACE. That never occurred to me, Rose.

ROSE. And you, Helga?

HELGA. Mama always said you changed the second you got your first period.

GRACE. Oh, good Lord, Helga –

HELGA. One minute you're miss sweetie pie. The next you're doing strange things…talking to yourself even. There's something's wrong with you I think.

GRACE. *(looking out a window, anxious to change the subject)* Look who's home…

ROSE. That makes everything real perfect, doesn't it, Mama?

GRACE. Don't say anything, Rose, if you can't say something nice.

ROSE. Oh, I assure you. I'll be quiet as a church mouse.

*(***YOUNG RUBY** *and* **WALTER** *enter.)*

WALTER. Ruby took good care of me, Grace. So don't go asking how things went.

GRACE. Aren't trucks wonderful?

WALTER. Nobody's been listening to the radio?

HELGA. Why are you asking about the radio?

WALTER. Apple juice on my hands. Itch like crazy.

(**WALTER** *turns and exits.*)

HELGA. Why is he asking if we've listened to the radio?
ROSE. Turn it on, Helga.
HELGA. *No.*
ROSE. Then I'll turn it on.
GRACE. You will not. Tonight we'll eat in peace.

(**FRIEDA** *enters.*)

FRIEDA. Everything's…all right?
GRACE. Would you surprise us for once? Say hello?
HELGA. Why wouldn't everything be all right?

(**FRIEDA** *crosses to the porch door, motioning to* **YOUNG RUBY** *who approaches.*)

FRIEDA. Mama wants me to be social – I try and I still get jumped on. So, I'm not saying anything to anybody… except *hello* …

(opening the door for **YOUNG RUBY***)*

And *goodbye.*

(**FRIEDA** *and* **YOUNG RUBY** *exit as* **ROSE** *steps to the radio.*)

HELGA. Who does she think she is, Mama?
GRACE. Oh, I think maybe the same person you were when you were her age.
ROSE. Mama, I want to listen to the radio…

(Lights are down on the parlor and up on the porch steps where **YOUNG RUBY** *sits alongside* **FRIEDA**.*)*

YOUNG RUBY. What's wrong?
FRIEDA. Good news first – Sid asked me out.
YOUNG RUBY. Oh, he does like you!
FRIEDA. Yeah, he likes me. I think he likes me a lot.
YOUNG RUBY. What about Pop?
FRIEDA. I should tell the handsomest man in the whole world, "Sorry. I can't go out with you until I'm fifty-two?"
YOUNG RUBY. You said "yes"?

FRIEDA. I said, "Sid, what took you so long?"
(pause)
Saturday...

YOUNG RUBY. Oh...

FRIEDA. A picture show...

YOUNG RUBY. Ohhh...

FRIEDA. In his car.

YOUNG RUBY. Ohhhh....

FRIEDA. Just the two of us.

YOUNG RUBY. *Alone* in his car! *Ohhhhhh...*

FRIEDA. *(after a moment, looking into the parlor)* They don't know, do they?

YOUNG RUBY. What are you talking about?

*(**HELGA** enters. She weeps openly. **GRACE** follows. She motions for **YOUNG RUBY** and **FRIEDA** to reenter the house which they do. A light focuses on **GRACE** who now cradles **HELGA** in her arms. Seconds later, **ROSE** appears. She crosses to a position behind **GRACE** and **HELGA**. Lights up on **ADULT RUBY**.)*

ADULT RUBY. Bulletins on radio that afternoon – stories Pop heard that morning at the market and Frieda overheard at work – told of an Allied invasion of France staged from bases in England. Because both Jimmy and Stan were in combat units there, Helga and Rose were certain they were involved and – by the time they had heard the reports, twelve hours or so after the first troops went ashore – were in the thick of battle and, at best, fighting for their lives. Believing her world had ended, Helga fell apart. Rose, on the other hand, surprised us...as she was increasingly inclined to do.

GRACE. Helga, sweetie. We don't know if Jimmy's involved even. Rose, tell her, we don't know if either boy is involved.

*(taking **HELGA** and **ROSE**'s hand, then bowing her head)*

Oh, dear Lord...be with them please...keep them safe...bring them home to us.

ROSE. He killed him.
GRACE. *Rose!*
ROSE. *Pop killed him!*
GRACE. Shame on you, Rose!
ROSE. *(mournfully as if the full impact of what she's said has hit her)* Stan is dead, Mama –
GRACE. No!
ROSE. *And he killed him!*
GRACE. No! No! *Nooooo!*

(GRACE reaches for ROSE who is not about to be comforted as the lights on them dim slowly to black, then come up on ADULT RUBY.)

ADULT RUBY. From the moment we heard reports of what would become known as D-Day, time stood still. Days passed, and the only letters Helga or Rose got were postmarked before June 6th. The anguish of not knowing – or worst, believing one of us knew something awful – overwhelmed us all. Only Frieda – now absorbed in her own world – more anxious than ever to escape to her job and budding romance – seemed immune.

(Lights up on FRIEDA and YOUNG RUBY who sit on a step of the porch It's the following Sunday.)

FRIEDA. God, I hate Sundays!
ADULT RUBY. And if only to escape my own reality, she had me as an eager audience.

(lights down on ADULT RUBY)

YOUNG RUBY. I *love* Sundays. It's the only day you don't work.
FRIEDA. Every night I say, "Dear God, let me work every day, especially Sundays."
YOUNG RUBY. Then I hope there's no god.
FRIEDA. Oh, there's a god all right. Only God could've created Sid.
YOUNG RUBY. When can I meet him?

FRIEDA. Some day I imagine.

YOUNG RUBY. I'll call him Mister Lazansky ...

FRIEDA. Don't be stupid.

YOUNG RUBY. I'll tell him I'm going to be that world-famous Rebecca Ruby some day. That'll impress him.

FRIEDA. Ruby!

YOUNG RUBY. Look at you, Frieda! *You're in love!*

FRIEDA. Shhh.

YOUNG RUBY. *(softly as she twirls around her sister, singing the words)* Frieda's in love. Frieda's in –

FRIEDA. You ever been kissed, Ruby?

YOUNG RUBY. That's none of your nosey business, Frieda!

FRIEDA. Of course, you haven't.

(suggestively)

Oh, Ruby...oh, my...oh, yes...

YOUNG RUBY. *(after a second, hoping **FRIEDA** will continue)* Well...?

FRIEDA. What?

YOUNG RUBY. What's it like...to be kissed...*by a man?*

FRIEDA. *Heaven!*

YOUNG RUBY. Hey, I've never been there either.

FRIEDA. You will! When he takes you into his arms. Puts his lips to yours, puts his hands –

YOUNG RUBY. *(putting her hands on her ears)* STOP!

FRIEDA. What's wrong with you?

YOUNG RUBY. I want to know everything...*except that everything.*

FRIEDA. I wasn't planning on telling *that everything.*

YOUNG RUBY. No, Frieda. You and Sid –

FRIEDA. Keep your mouth shut.

(pause)

There's something else...Sid is Jewish.

YOUNG RUBY. Jewish? You mean – ?

FRIEDA. Jewish! Jewish! Yes! Yes!

YOUNG RUBY. Oh, you're dead!

FRIEDA. What Pop says about Jews – it's crazy. You know that!

YOUNG RUBY. You're really scaring me, Frieda.

FRIEDA. He's rich – at least his father's rich. He's beautiful. He's educated. He's got a deferment –

YOUNG RUBY. *He's Jewish, Frieda!*

FRIEDA. Yes, he is. And I love him.

*(**FRIEDA** turns to **RUBY** and stares. **RUBY** looks back, not knowing what, if anything to say. The lights slowly dim to black.)*

*(The parlor, the next day or so. **GRACE** sits in an arm chair, busily sewing. Meanwhile, **HELGA** is back at her desk, writing what appears to be another letter. **GRACE** glances at her a few times before speaking.)*

GRACE. Florence Synderkamp told me a funny Omar Zelch story yesterday. I promised her I wouldn't tell anybody…

*(**GRACE** waits for **HELGA** to continue; **HELGA** doesn't.)*

One minute he's plowing his field…the next his overalls get caught in the horse's reins. Down Omar goes. Next thing, they've started slipping off – one leg at a time. In a wink, Omar Henry Zelch is naked from his belly button to his boots – in the light of the noon-day sun – chasing his mule…

(softly to make sure no one else can hear)

All the time holding his vitals as if they were the keys to the kingdom or something. Of course, Florence Synderkamp also claims she saw our Lord and Savior buying paint – bright yellow she swears – at the Sears-Roebuck on the Fourth of July.

*(Silence as **GRACE** watches **HELGA** continue to write.)*

There's something I don't understand.

*(Still no responds from **HELGA**.)*

I'll just mind my own business.

HELGA. What, Mama?

GRACE. Nothing important really…

HELGA. What don't you understand, Mama?

GRACE. I guess I don't understand your letters. You keep writing them, but you don't mail most of them – not anymore I don't think.

*(Realizes she's afraid to hear **HELGA**'s answer.)*

I'm getting myself lemonade.

HELGA. You know why, Mama?

GRACE. I'll bring you a big glass.

(crossing to get the lemonade)

HELGA. Mama, I need to tell you something.

GRACE. If it's something I don't want to hear –

HELGA. I had a dream. About Jimmy – a terrible, awful dream.

GRACE. Dreams are dreams –

HELGA. He went ashore, like I thought –

GRACE. – They don't mean anything.

HELGA. All of a sudden, he was…

(beat)

He was real still. What was left of him, was real still.

GRACE. Sweetie – no.

HELGA. It keeps coming back – over and over. And I think it's telling me something. Mama, I think maybe Jimmy's…dead.

GRACE. No, no, sweetie. A bad dream – that's all it was – just an awful, terrible dream.

*(**GRACE** comforts **HELGA**. We hear **HELGA**'s soft sobs as the lights dim on them and come up on **ADULT RUBY**.)*

ADULT RUBY. Growing up, all of us – even Frieda – would confess our fears to Mama and once heard by her, like magic, they'd disappear. But Helga's fears and Rose's too – as irrational as they seemed – were different. All of Mama's hugs and promises couldn't make either of

them believe the sun would shine again. For them –
and Mama and Pop too – the wait for news – any news
– was an awful burden.

(Lights slowly come up on **FRIEDA** *[who stands] and*
SID *[who sits]. It is the next afternoon, and they're in*
WALTER's *orchard, a setting created by lighting.* **ADULT**
RUBY *turns to the pair as she speaks.)*

ADULT RUBY. And then there was Frieda. If she worried about what might be around the corner, she kept it a secret. Just as she was determined to keep Sid's existence a secret from everybody but me.

(Lights down on **ADULT RUBY** *and up fully on* **SID** *and*
FRIEDA. **SID** *is a nice looking, confident young man.*
FRIEDA *appears nervous.)*

SID. Sit down. I'm not going to bite, Frieda.

FRIEDA. Thanks for bringing me home, but maybe…

(looking toward the house)

Before somebody sees us…maybe you should go, huh?

SID. Sit with me, Frieda.

FRIEDA. All right. But just for a minute.

(Sits down several feet from **SID***; she remains anxious.)*

You'll be pleased I think. I told Ruby about you.

SID. Somebody in your family knows Sid Lazansky exists. You have gifted me, Frieda.

FRIEDA. She's dying to meet you –

SID. Your folks, however, don't have any idea –

FRIEDA. Actually I've got three sisters…Ruby, Helga –

SID. And Rose. I know, Frieda. And a mother and father I assume. So when do I meet them?

FRIEDA. Oh, you will!

SID. Tonight?

FRIEDA. Not tonight! Some other night.

*(***SID** *moves closer to* **FRIEDA***; he takes her hand.)*

SID. I embarrass you. That's it, isn't it?

FRIEDA. No, you don't embarrass me!

SID. Then why haven't you introduced me? I don't understand.

FRIEDA. Really...I think I should go inside.

SID. Maybe I do understand ...

(**FRIEDA** *stands.*)

Because I'm not off fighting the war somewhere –

FRIEDA. You're deferred, Sid. You can't help it if you're deferred –

SID. That's what I thought. It's reason number two.

FRIEDA. Reason number two?

SID. I'm Jewish.

FRIEDA. *That is ridiculous!* Now I'm really going inside. Good night...

(*takes another couple of steps toward the house*)

SID. Wait...

(**FRIEDA** *stops.*)

Take my hand, Frieda...

(**SID** – *still sitting* – *extends his hand to* **FRIEDA**; *she doesn't take it.*)

Take it please! Pull me up.

(**FRIEDA**, *somewhat reluctantly, takes* **SID**'s *hand, attempts to pull him to his feet.*)

I'm going with you.

FRIEDA. Inside...?

(*Quickly drops* **SID**'s *hand, causing* **SID** *to fall back.*)

No!

SID. *Yes!*

FRIEDA. *No, I said!*

SID. Hey, I've got it all worked out. I'll march in...I'll say, "Mr. and Mrs. Zweifel, my name is Sid Lazansky. I think maybe you'd like to meet me...*since I'm falling in love with you wonderful, beautiful daughter.*"

(**FRIEDA** *steps back to* **SID**, *pulling him to a standing position, then leads him by the hand away from the house.*)

SID. The house…it's the other way.…

(**FRIEDA** *stops, takes* **SID** *into her arms and gives him a kiss he'll remember. Upon breaking the embrace, she again leads him by the hand away from the house.*)

Okay. All right. This time you win. Next time, I do.

(**FRIEDA** *continues to pull* **SID** *away from the house as the lights dim.*)

(*A little later that same evening. When the lights come back up, they're on* **WALTER** – *who sits in his chair and appears to be asleep* – *and* **GRACE** – *who sits close to the radio which is on; the volume is low.*)

RADIO ANNOUNCER. "In France, reports indicate that Allied forces now control eighty miles of the Normandy coast. Earlier today, General Eisenhower released a message congratulating Allied troops. At the same time, he warned of bitter fighting ahead…"

WALTER. Sneaking a listen, huh?

GRACE. (*turns off the radio*) You startled me, Walter.

WALTER. First it was the war reports. Now it's music…no Fibber McGee and Molly…no nothing –

GRACE. We could always try talking to each other, Walter.

(*In spite of* **GRACE**'s *comment, neither speak for a period. After a second,* **WALTER** *closes his eyes.*)

I made a good lunch today. Swiss steak, like you like. You didn't show up, I thought about bringing it to you in the orchard.

(**GRACE** *looks to* **WALTER**, *hoping for a response. There isn't one.*)

At least Frieda will have a nice supper…she gets home from working overtime again.

(*pause*)

GRACE Can I tell you something, Walter – before you fall asleep? Something Helga told me, without you getting all worked up?

(**WALTER** *doesn't respond.*)

Walter, I need you to look at me....

WALTER. *(His eyes remain closed.)* You were talking about Helga.

GRACE. Oh, Walter! She's having dreams. About Jimmy – nightmares really.

WALTER. He's dead.

GRACE. *What?*

WALTER. In her dreams...Jimmy's dead.

GRACE. How did you – ?

WALTER. That's Helga.

GRACE. Oh, Walter. You don't give her any credit. You don't give any of the girls any credit, do you? What's wrong with you? We use to laugh. With the girls, we'd laugh. What happened to make you so...cold?

(beat)

I have them too, Walter...terrible nightmares.

WALTER. *(painfully)* Nightmares, Grace...

GRACE. What...?

WALTER. ...I know nightmares.

GRACE. Walter...

(**WALTER** *shakes his head as* **GRACE** *looks into his eyes. She can see tears.*)

Talk to me, Walter. Tell me everything's going to be all right.

(beat)

Walter, everything is going to be all right, isn't it?

(After a moment of silence, **GRACE** *crosses to the door exiting to the porch. As she does, lights also come up on* **ADULT RUBY**. **GRACE** *opens the door, steps out, pausing on the top step. In the dark, she's barely visible.)*

ADULT RUBY. If some people are thinkers and some are talkers, Pop was a thinker. Unfortunately, he rarely told us much of what he was thinking. Mama knew that, of course. So she'd made excuses for him, telling anybody who would listen, that that's what happens when you shared five rooms with five women. But he was never as withdrawn as he was that summer, and none of us understood...especially Mama who tried to avoid confrontation as if it were the ultimate evil ...

(GRACE hears FRIEDA's voice in the distance. The lights begin to come down on ADULT RUBY.)

FRIEDA. *(offstage)* Stop...!

ADULT RUBY. *(looking in the direction of the sounds)* Some confrontations, however, were impossible to avoid...even for her.

FRIEDA. *(offstage)* Sid, I said no! Sid...please!

(After a moment, we hear the slam of a car door.)

I still love you...see you tomorrow...bye-bye... drive careful...bye.

(FRIEDA comes into view. We hear the sound of a car disappearing into the distance. As she approaches the house and GRACE – who stands in the shadows – FRIEDA tucks her blouse into her skirt. She all but bumps into GRACE.)

GRACE. Who's Sid, Frieda?

FRIEDA. *Mama!* You scared me.

GRACE. The man you were talking to – with the car. Who is he?

FRIEDA. Nobody, Mama.

GRACE. Nobody?

FRIEDA. Just a man.

GRACE. Just a man, huh?

FRIEDA. He works at the plant. He gave me a ride home – that's all.

(She begins to ascend the porch steps.)

Mama, I'm starving.

GRACE. Do you tell every man you know you love him?

(*FRIEDA attempts to step by GRACE. She takes FRIEDA's hand.*)

Frieda! Who is he?

FRIEDA. Mama, I'm almost twenty –

GRACE. *Frieda, who's Sid?*

FRIEDA. He's a man. And I guess...well, I like him – kind of.

GRACE. A boyfriend?

FRIEDA. Sort of, I guess.

GRACE. With a car? How long has this been going on?

FRIEDA. I'll fix my own supper.

(*Again FRIEDA attempts to enter the house; GRACE again stops her.*)

GRACE. *How long has this been going on?*

FRIEDA. Mama! *Nothing is going on!*

GRACE. You know what happens, Frieda –

FRIEDA. *Mama, I told you...nothing's going on!*

GRACE. (*with difficulty, crossing her arms over her chest*) I don't want you seeing him again.

FRIEDA. *Mama, no!*

GRACE. I don't want you going out with him again.

FRIEDA. I can't do that, Mama.

GRACE. Something happens, Rose –

FRIEDA. It's nothing like that. Listen to me. It's nothing like that.

GRACE. What's his name?

FRIEDA. Sid. You know that.

GRACE. His last name?

FRIEDA. His last name is...Smith.

GRACE. Oh, Frieda...

FRIEDA. He's got flat feet. His daddy works for the railroad. Anything else you'd like to know?

GRACE. You wouldn't lie to me?

FRIEDA. Of course not – no, Mama.

(FRIEDA embraces GRACE.)

He's just a good friend, Mama…nothing more.

GRACE. Just a friend?

FRIEDA. A friend – that's all – I promise.

(GRACE and FRIEDA look at one another as lights come down on the porch and up in the parlor where WALTER is asleep in his chair. After a second, FRIEDA enters.)

(sarcastically, as she passes his father) Pop.

(FRIEDA exits as GRACE re-enters. She takes a light afghan, then carefully drapes it over WALTER. As she's does, ROSE, dressed in a robe, enters.)

ROSE. You're too good to him, Mama.

GRACE. He gets in bed, he can't breathe right. If it helps him to sleep sitting up, I don't mind. Can I get you a glass of milk maybe?

ROSE. *(shaking her head)* I'll just sit here a minute. Turn out the light, if you want.

GRACE. Tsk, just sit in the dark.

ROSE. For a minute.

GRACE. Honey, go outside. It's plenty dark out there.

ROSE. Don't worry, Mama…I wouldn't dare wake the man.

GRACE. He's worked in his orchard all day, Rose. Be quiet… please.

(GRACE turns off the floor lamp. The room is dark, but not so dark that we can't see ROSE's movements.)

ROSE. Good night, Mama.

GRACE. Good night, Rose.

(GRACE repositions the afghan on WALTER, then exits. After a long moment, ROSE rises and walks slowly to the radio. She turns it on; the volume is down. We hear "Sentimental Journey" or a similar tune from the 40s. After a moment, ROSE begins dancing around the room, extending her arm as if she were waltzing with someone

very special, perhaps humming to herself as she moves. After a few revolutions, she bumps into a small table. It crashes to the floor. **WALTER** *awakens.)*

WALTER. *What's the...?*

(**WALTER** *reaches up to the floor lamp, turning it on; he sees* **ROSE** *who continues to dance.)*

What are you doing, Rose?

ROSE. Isn't it obvious what we're doing...?

(Steps up the pace, now dancing with a flair.)

We're dancing the night away. And don't we do it beautifully? Fred and Ginger of the Farmers' Club set. That good, aren't we, Pop? One-two-three...one-two-three. Gracefully, we sail across the dance floor...everybody's eyes riveted on us...especially yours...one-two –

WALTER. Stop it, Rose!

ROSE. But yours aren't smiling. Is that rage I see? One-two-three...

WALTER. *Grace...*

ROSE. Because I'm dancing with Stan.

WALTER. *Stop it!*

ROSE. You don't approve. And why don't you approve? One-two-three. Because he's Polish? Because he loves me? Because he's asked me to marry him?

(**WALTER** *crosses to the radio.)*

Or because he told you your man with the mustache... *is a monster!*

(**WALTER** *turns off the radio;* **ROSE** *stops dancing, immediately raises her right arm in the Nazi salute. Her voice resounds in the abrupt silence.)*

SEIG HEIL...SEIG HIEL!!

WALTER. *GRACE...*

ROSE. Which one was it, Pop?

WALTER. Please go to your room, Rose.

ROSE. All of the above maybe?

(**GRACE** *enters, wearing a robe.* **ROSE** *sees her.*)

ROSE. My father thinks I'm a child again…

GRACE. Oh, Rose. I begged you to hold your tongue.

WALTER. *(to* **ROSE***)* What do you want me to say?

GRACE. Go to bed, Rose – please.

WALTER. *(to* **GRACE***; he's becoming very agitated)* I don't know what she wants me to say!

ROSE. I want to hear you say, "You're sorry"!

GRACE. *(sensing* **WALTER***'s breathing difficulty)* Take deep breaths, Walter.

ROSE. I want to hear him say –

GRACE. No more, Rose!

ROSE. I want to hear him say, "Rose, I'm sorry…I ruined your life."

GRACE. *How awful, Rose!*

ROSE. I'm waiting, Pop. Tell me you know what you've done to me.

GRACE. She's talking about Stan, I think. Rose, are you talking about Stan?

ROSE. I'm listening, Pop…I don't hear anything…

GRACE. Stan's coming back.

ROSE. What, Mama?

GRACE. I said Stan will come home…here.

ROSE. He would've come back to me?

GRACE. Yes, of course, Rose…he'll come back to you.

ROSE. Then he really loved me?

GRACE. Yes, yes! He loves you! Walter, tell her Stan loves her.

ROSE. *Then it's true.*

GRACE. What's true?

ROSE. IT'S TRUE…!

GRACE. Walter, do you understand what she's saying?

ROSE. *HE RUINED MY LIFE.*

(**ROSE** *looks directly at* **WALTER**, *who looks away.* **ROSE** *resumes dancing, her arm once again extended.*)

ROSE. Oh, didn't we dance beautifully, Mama? For a moment there, weren't we something?...One-two-three, one-two-three, one-two-three...

(**GRACE** *watches in stunned silence as* **ROSE** – *in her own world now and very much alone* – *negotiates the parlor floor as the lights slowly dim to black.*)

End of Act One

ACT TWO

(The parlor, two weeks later. At rise, lights come up, revealing **ADULT RUBY**. *She sits in a chair and looks at the album. After a moment, she stands, strolls through the room, stops. She turns to the audience, speaking as Edward R. Murrow might have spoken.)*

ADULT RUBY. Just because a war is fought halfway around the world…does not mean there are no casualties at home.

(pause, managing a smile)

Of course, Edward R. Murrow would've phrased it more eloquently. But it was true. During that summer, bombs fell and cannons fired half a world away. Yet here – seemingly sheltered by our mountains – war had taken an awful toll on us as well. Three weeks after D-Day – still without a letter – Rose and Helga were more convinced than ever that Stan and Jimmy were battlefield casualties. Frieda – who used her job in Bluefield to escape the conflict at home – continued her relationship with someone I was sure Pop, failing heart and all, would never accept.

(Lights come up on **GRACE** *who sits on a porch step.* **YOUNG RUBY** *sits alongside.)*

And, then there was Mama…as determined as ever to pick up the pieces. Which by then were as shattered as her cherished blue and white Thanksgiving platter.

GRACE. Delores Munslinger got a good-news telegram this morning. Her boy Eugene. You remember him, Ruby – the girls teased him about his ears being big.

(remembering, a slight chuckle)

GRACE. Helga – shame on her – claimed you couldn't say anything about Eugene Munslinger – especially about his ears – without him hearing you. Dolores' news was he'd been wounded.

YOUNG RUBY. That's awful news, Mama!

GRACE. The boy's alive, Ruby. He's coming home. I thought about telling Helga. Rose, too. I don't think I will.

YOUNG RUBY. Helga would cry, I think.

GRACE. And Rose…Well anymore, I don't know what Rose would do. So, I'll keep my mouth shut, say my prayers. I'm beginning to think maybe I should pray all the time – like my Aunt Lulu.

YOUNG RUBY. She prayed all the time?

GRACE. Aunt Lulu, bless her heart, never talked to anybody but God. Now, that's not exactly true. Once – down on her knees, in the middle of asking the Lord for another big-time miracle – she asked me to pass her a glass of water. I came this close to saying, "Come on, Aunt Lulu…ask God for something easy for a change…ask *Him* to pass you the water."

YOUNG RUBY. You still tell funny stories, Mama.

GRACE. Well, it wasn't funny what happened to her.

YOUNG RUBY. What?

GRACE. One Aunt Lulu story is more than enough.

YOUNG RUBY. Really, what happened to her, Mama?

GRACE. Well, they committed her – that's what happened to her.

YOUNG RUBY. Because she prayed all the time?

GRACE. Because she prayed her neighbor's house would burn down. When God didn't do it, she did.

YOUNG RUBY. *(laughing)* Oh, Mama…

GRACE. Don't get me started on Aunt Lulu stories.

YOUNG RUBY. Maybe that's what we need, huh?

GRACE. I keep telling myself, Ruby…everything's going to work out okay.

YOUNG RUBY. It will, Mama. You'll see.

GRACE. Then why do I worry so? Try to sleep, end up walking the floor? Try to think about what's for supper, end up thinking about Rose, your daddy, Helga? Now it's Frieda –

YOUNG RUBY. Frieda?

GRACE. Do I need to worry about her too?

YOUNG RUBY. What are you asking me, Mama?

GRACE. She's got a boyfriend – I know you know that. Is he a nice boy?

YOUNG RUBY. I guess so – sure.

GRACE. Sid – that's his name, isn't it?

YOUNG RUBY. Sid something or the other.

GRACE. Brown or Smith – something like that maybe?

YOUNG RUBY. It's a real funny-sounding name.

(From **GRACE***'s reaction,* **RUBY** *senses something is wrong.)*

GRACE. Oh, dear Lord, watch over all of them please. Frieda especially.

(In the distance, we hear music – up tempo big band sounds that contrast sharply with **GRACE***'s depression. The lights on* **GRACE** *and* **YOUNG RUBY** *dim slowly to black and come up on* **ADULT RUBY***.)*

ADULT RUBY. I wasn't a worrier like Mama and Helga. Still, that summer I had more than my share of concerns, and Mama – reeling from everything that had happened and fearing that even worse news was around the corner – had worked her way to the top of my list. So, I decided I'd help, and I'd begin with Frieda…

(Lights down on **ADULT RUBY** *and up some on* **YOUNG RUBY***. She sits on a porch step, looking intently into the darkness. The music – it comes from a car radio – continues. We hear the added sounds of a car door shutting, followed by the acceleration of the vehicle. Music and sounds are down, then out, as* **FRIEDA** *comes into view.* **FRIEDA** *sees* **YOUNG RUBY** *as she approaches.)*

FRIEDA. Whatdaya think you're doing?

YOUNG RUBY. Whatdaya think I'm doing?

FRIEDA. Spying – that's what you're doing!

YOUNG RUBY. Really, I was just sitting here –

FRIEDA. Yeah, I bet.

YOUNG RUBY. *Watching you neck!!*

FRIEDA. How dare you!

YOUNG RUBY. *Shame on you, Frieda!*

FRIEDA. Mind your own damn business, Ruby!

YOUNG RUBY. I keep thinking about your friend Alice Schneider.

FRIEDA. Shut your filthy chops too!

YOUNG RUBY. How do you know you won't end up like her?

FRIEDA. Because I won't!

YOUNG RUBY. If you do, will you marry him?

FRIEDA. What's got into you?

YOUNG RUBY. I forgot. You can't marry him.

FRIEDA. I promise you, Ruby! Pop isn't picking my husband –

YOUNG RUBY. *Sid's Jewish, Frieda!*

FRIEDA. I'll marry anybody I want – *even if he's Jewish!*

YOUNG RUBY. What if he doesn't ask you – *because you're not Jewish?*

FRIEDA. Thanks a million, Ruby.

(She ascends a couple of steps.)

YOUNG RUBY. Stop. I need a favor.

FRIEDA. Forget it.

YOUNG RUBY. For Mama. She knows about Sid –

FRIEDA. So…?

YOUNG RUBY. She's worried sick about things nobody can do anything about. Don't make her worry about you too…

FRIEDA. God, I've ended up with two mothers.

YOUNG RUBY. Be careful – okay?

FRIEDA. Sure.

YOUNG RUBY. Promise?

FRIEDA. Promise to stay out of my business?

YOUNG RUBY. Stop necking in front of everybody!

FRIEDA. Makes you jealous, huh? Makes you want to grow up, doesn't it? Well, eat your heart out, *little sister!*

*(**FRIEDA** opens the porch door and is about to enter the house.)*

YOUNG RUBY. If you don't do anything else…

FRIEDA. Yeah?

YOUNG RUBY. Pray for Mama. I think she's going to need it.

*(The following morning. Lights down on **FRIEDA** and **YOUNG RUBY** and up immediately on **ADULT RUBY** who stands up left and **ROSE** who is alone in the parlor; **ROSE** stares at an envelope in her hand.)*

ADULT RUBY. On the morning of June the 25th, 1944, Rose received a letter.

*(**ROSE** hesitantly opens the envelope, removes the letter and studies it as **ADULT RUBY** speaks.)*

It consisted of a single page, dated June the 10th… mailed – as it turned out – from a military hospital in a place called Croyden, England. She knew the letter pertained to Stan, but it had been written in Polish… until she could get a translation, she wouldn't know what it said.

*(**GRACE** enters. **ROSE** sees her and quickly refolds the letter, putting it out of sight. As she does, lights on **ADULT RUBY** begin to dim.)*

ADULT RUBY. Until then – until she knew Stan's fate for sure – she was determined to keep it a secret…even from Mama.

GRACE. Please tell me you're feeling better, honey.

*(**ROSE** doesn't respond; her mind is elsewhere throughout this sequence.)*

Rose, I asked if you're feeling better?

ROSE. It comes and goes.

GRACE. You ask me, it comes more than it goes. The problem is you don't eat right.

ROSE. Is that's my problem, Mama?

GRACE. *(making an effort to cheer* **ROSE***)* If you don't eat right, your teeth'll fall out. Of course, then you'll have an excuse for not eating right.

ROSE. No stories, Mama!

GRACE. That's what happened to my Uncle Henry. The man ate nothing but corn on the cob. Two ears for breakfast, three for –

ROSE. *Stop it, Mama!*

GRACE. First his face broke out. Then his hair fell out. Then his teeth were gone and – without his front teeth to eat the wrong food with – well, you can imagine what happened next. The lesson is...nobody can survive on tea and toast alone.

(**ROSE** *covers her ears with her hands.*)

And while I'm saying things you don't want to hear, you cannot spend day and night shut up in that room –

ROSE. MAMA, LOOK WHERE I AM. I'M WHERE YOU WANT ME. ISN'T THIS WHERE YOU WANT ME?

GRACE. Don't shout at me, Rose.

(*pause*)

I saw the mailman leaving. Nothing again I suppose?

(**ROSE** *doesn't respond.*)

Fortunately there's something in the Bible about patience. I'll look it up for you –

ROSE. *No, Mama.*

GRACE. I'll look it up for myself.

(*Picking up a Bible, flipping through the pages, then stopping mid-way through.*)

Tsk. The 23rd Psalm – I had to recite it at my confirmation graduation. Oh, I got so nervous, Rose. Instead of saying, "Thy rod and thy staff, they *comfort* me," I said, "Thy rod and thy staff, they *support* me." Everybody laughed themselves silly –

ROSE. *I don't care!*

GRACE. Well, Reverend Bauer sure did. He made me write all six verses a hundred times.

(GRACE continues looking through the Bible as FRIEDA enters. She's unusually well dressed. GRACE is surprised to see her.)

GRACE. Frieda ...

FRIEDA. Morning, Mama...

GRACE. I thought you'd left hours ago.

FRIEDA. I...overslept I guess.

GRACE. Got yourself all dolled up too.

FRIEDA. I wanted to look nice.

GRACE. To work in a factory.

FRIEDA. I'm late tonight, don't worry. Okay?

GRACE. Rose, did you know Frieda has a boyfriend?

FRIEDA. Mama...!

GRACE. What's his name, sweetie?

FRIEDA. Mama, we've had this conversation.

GRACE. What's his name, Frieda?

FRIEDA. I told you, Mama.

GRACE. *(to ROSE)* We know his first name is Sid. We're just not real sure what his last name is, are we, Frieda?

ROSE. Is he special, Frieda?

FRIEDA. Maybe a little...

ROSE. *(to FRIEDA)* If he's special, don't let him go.

GRACE. What are you saying, Rose?

ROSE. If he's special, don't let him out of your sight!

GRACE. Frieda's nineteen years old – !

ROSE. *If you love him, Frieda, don't let him go!*

GRACE. *She doesn't love him, Rose!* Honey, you don't really love him, do you?

ROSE. *Listen to what I'm saying, Frieda!*

GRACE. *(all but shoving FRIEDA out the door)* Frieda, go on.

ROSE. You'll end up like me.

GRACE. *Frieda, go on!*

*(With **GRACE**'s help, **FRIEDA** exits. **ROSE** crosses to the door.)*

ROSE. *Listen to me, Frieda!* DON'T LET HIM GO!

GRACE. Don't do this to yourself, Rose – I beg you. Don't do this to either of us.

*(**GRACE** attempts to comfort **ROSE**, who looks at the audience as if a suppressed memory has flashed into her mind. The lights slowly dim to black. In the dark, we hear a voice of a railroad conductor.)*

CONDUCTOR. *Now boarding…on Platform Number One…for Beckley, Clarksburg, Morgantown and points north …*

*(When lights return, it's early February, 1944. **STAN** and **ROSE** stand on railroad platform, a space created entirely by light and sound. **ROSE** is weeping. Both wear heavy winter coats. We hear a train whistle.)*

STAN. Rose. I asked you…please do not cry.

*(**ROSE** wants to say something. Before she can, **STAN** put a a finger on her lips.)*

Shhh…

*(wipes a tear from **ROSE**'s cheek)*

Your smile – I want to remember your smile.

*(**ROSE** forces a smile; **STAN** likes what he sees.)*

That is the Rose I want to come home to.

ROSE. You will come home?

STAN. My darling, Rose –

ROSE. To me?

STAN. – How many times must I tell you – ?

ROSE. Tell me again.

STAN. *(smiles, nods, wiping another tear from **ROSE**'s cheek)* I will go to war –

ROSE. It's not *your* war!

STAN. It *is* my war!

*(**ROSE** shakes her head repeatedly.)*

My, sweet…sweet, Rose. We have talked about this so many times

(takes her hand, tenderly)

It is over – the war is done. At this very spot, I will step off this very train. I will search for you. I will find you. I will run to you, take you into my arms –

*(**STAN** takes **ROSE** into his arms. They kiss long and passionately.)*

CONDUCTOR. Last call for Beckley, Clarksburg, Morgantown. All aboard!

*(**STAN** breaks the embrace, smiles at **ROSE** for a moment, then begins to back away.)*

ROSE. No!

(She takes a few steps after him, then stops.)

Stan…no! Please…! Don't go…! Nooo…!

*(**STAN** says something to **ROSE**. Because his words are drowned out by the shrill sound of a locomotive whistle, neither she nor we know what they are. In a flash, **STAN** is gone and **ROSE** is left very much alone. Blackout.)*

*(Lights come up on **ADULT RUBY**. It is the day after **ROSE** and **FRIEDA**'s encounter.)*

ADULT RUBY. Helga, I'm certain, prayed that news about Jimmy would arrive in a letter written by him from somewhere in France. It would tell her he had survived the invasion, and – for him – the worst was over. Like so many events back then, it didn't happen that way, and Pop was the first to know. Alone in his orchard on that hot late-June morning, he saw the Western Union driver pull up. Whether by desire or obligation, he signed for the delivery…a small yellow envelope containing a telegram addressed to Mrs. James L. Nelander. I can only imagine what was going through his mind as he entered the parlor…the unopened telegram in hand…in search of Helga.

*(As **ADULT RUBY** speaks, **WALTER** enters from the porch. In his hand is a small yellow envelope. A moment later, **GRACE** also enters. She sees the telegram and gasps. Lights down on **ADULT RUBY**.)*

WALTER. I guess…you should get her.

GRACE. Who, Walter?

WALTER. *(hesitating, looking up at **GRACE**)* Helga.

GRACE. Jimmy…*noooo…*

(sits because she can no longer stand)

*(Silence. After a few moments, **WALTER** crosses to the door leading to the back bedrooms. **GRACE** watches him through fear-filled, tear-filled eyes as he opens the door and exits the parlor. Seconds later, he reenters without the telegram. His eyes lock on **GRACE**'s eyes as he crosses to the center of the room. He sits. After a few painful moments, **GRACE** – realizing she should be with **HELGA** – struggles to her feet and, with difficulty, takes several steps toward **HELGA**'s bedroom. Before she can exit the parlor, **HELGA** enters. The telegram – now open – is in her hand. **GRACE** and **WALTER** look at her in fearful anticipation. She returns their gaze for a long agonizing moment.)*

HELGA. He's okay.

GRACE. *Oh, thank God.* Walter! Jimmy's okay!

*(**GRACE** rushes to **HELGA**; they embrace and share tears.)*

HELGA. He's in a hospital. In England. But he's alive!

GRACE. *Hallelujah –*

HELGA. *(a sudden realization)* But, Mama! He's wounded…

GRACE. He made it, Helga! He'll come home! *Honey, your husband's coming home!*

*(**HELGA** rushes to **WALTER** and she gives him a hug which he returns.)*

HELGA. Pop, Jimmy made it!

(looking Heavenward)

Thank you, Lord!

*(**ROSE** enters to see the celebration.)*

GRACE. Helga, tell your sister your good news.

HELGA. Jimmy's in a hospital in England. But he'll be okay…that's what it says.

(waving the telegram, attempting to hold back her tears)

GRACE. Isn't that good news, Rose?

*(A brief silence as **WALTER**, **GRACE** and **HELGA** look at **ROSE**.)*

Rose, did you hear Helga?

*(**ROSE** doesn't answer. Instead she turns and crosses to a door.)*

Rose, sweetie – this is just the beginning of our good news. I can feel it. Can't you feel it, Rose?

*(Without speaking, **ROSE** exits; **GRACE** now turns to **WALTER** for assurance.)*

Can't you feel it, Walter?

(All look at one another as the lights slowly dim to black.)

*(That evening. Late. **GRACE** and **WALTER** are in the parlor; **GRACE** knits while **WALTER** appears asleep. After a few seconds, **HELGA** enters. She's dressed in a robe. They speak softly so as not to disturb **WALTER**.)*

HELGA. I thought I'd sleep like a baby tonight.

GRACE. But your mind's buzzing, and your eyes are doing the polka.

HELGA. The jitterbug, I think

GRACE. Oh, Helga. You *are* my daughter!

*(looks at **WALTER**)*

Your father, however, falls asleep at noon…walking behind his mule…in the rain.

WALTER. I hear you, Grace.

GRACE. If you're still awake, Walter, Frieda will be home soon. So mind your business please.

HELGA. Rose's reaction disappointed me, Mama.

GRACE. When Rose gets good news, she'll celebrate too.

HELGA. She was sick again this morning.

GRACE. Worry makes us that way, sweetie.

HELGA. She disappeared for hours this afternoon.

GRACE. Will you quit! She took a walk – I saw her myself…

(crosses to a cabinet, opens the door, begins searching)

Now, we haven't had a celebration in this house since our tenth anniversary. So…we are celebrating tonight. Where is that bottle of wine…?

(chuckling)

Folks from church came over. In a wink everybody got to drinking punch, carrying on like you wouldn't believe. Especially old Henry Nostmeyer who wouldn't say ten words to save his soul. But there he was…standing in the middle of our kitchen table, reciting – of all the crazy things – "The Gettysburg Address." Only he couldn't get "four score and seven" out of his mouth straight. The next morning I found out why…your church-going Daddy poured wine in the punch, then served it to souls who thought liquor was the work of the devil. I could've shot the man…until I remembered how much fun everybody had. Tsk, nothing in here stronger than maple syrup.

*(**FRIEDA** enters. Although presentable, she's not put together as well as she might like, perhaps because she's had a sip or two of something stronger than maple syrup.)*

GRACE. Look who's home.

*(looks at **WALTER** who appears to be asleep)*

Right on schedule, too.

FRIEDA. What's going on?

GRACE. We've got good news!

FRIEDA. Okay.

HELGA. Jimmy's been wounded, but not so bad. He's in a hospital in England –

GRACE. Honey, Jimmy made it through the invasion. He's going to be okay.

FRIEDA. Okay!

HELGA. Is that all you can say?

FRIEDA. Good news I guess…yeah.

*(**FRIEDA** takes a couple of steps and trips over a chair. **WALTER** opens his eyes. **GRACE** sees him look at **FRIEDA**.)*

GRACE. Frieda, go on to bed.

WALTER. *(sitting up in the chair)* Give your pop a goodnight kiss.

GRACE.	**FRIEDA.**
Walter.	NO.

GRACE. She's just tired, Walter.

WALTER. Here, on the cheek.

GRACE. She's wants to go to bed.

WALTER. *She's drunk!*

FRIEDA. I am not…*drunk*.

WALTER. Smell her breath!

GRACE.	**HELGA.**
I will not.	Just go to bed, Frieda.

WALTER. Where have you been?

FRIEDA. Working overtime…

WALTER. Don't lie to me.

FRIEDA. Until somebody gave me a beer. Which I drank. Then I had another –

GRACE. Oh, Frieda…

FRIEDA. Too bad you don't like it…Pop!

HELGA. *(attempting to escort **FRIEDA** from the room)* Let's go –

FRIEDA. *(pulling away from **HELGA**)* Helga, let me go!

WALTER. Get her to bed, Grace.

FRIEDA. I have something to say –

HELGA. Help me, Mama.

*(**GRACE** crosses to **FRIEDA**. She and **HELGA** attempt to escort **FRIEDA** from the room; **HELGA** resists.)*

FRIEDA. A big secret – that's what I want to tell him.
GRACE. Hush, Frieda.
FRIEDA. I'm in love, Pop.
GRACE. Go to bed, Frieda!
FRIEDA. Mama, it's okay. You'll like him. But him…

(points to **WALTER***)*

Oh, I don't think so.

WALTER. What's she talking about, Grace?
FRIEDA. Tell him, Mama.
GRACE. Just a friend, Walter. Nothing to get upset about.
FRIEDA. That's not true, Mama. He's not just a friend…
GRACE. No more, Frieda!
FRIEDA. And his name's not Smith.
GRACE. Frieda, no!

*(***FRIEDA*** continues to resist any effort to escort her from the room.)*

FRIEDA. Something really big is happening here, Pop. Your daughter…Frieda Frances Zweifel…is madly, passionately in love. And ready or not…his name is Sidney Abraham *Lazansky*.

(Lights come up on **ADULT RUBY** *as* **HELGA** *successfully escorts* **FRIEDA** *from the parlor. As* **ADULT RUBY** *speaks,* **WALTER** *and* **GRACE** *stand facing one another; although neither speak, we sense the sadness and desperation they share.)*

ADULT RUBY. The next morning, when I heard what Frieda had said, I knew our relationship would never be the same. While I was still stumbling through adolescence, Frieda had charged fearlessly into adulthood and – in her mind at least – the two no longer mixed. Mama, who had begun to believe the sun might once again shine, was suddenly and ruefully made aware the clouds were as thick ever. And Pop – whether he admitted it to himself or not – received the clearest message of all…his dominion over us was rushing to a speedy end.

(Lights down on **ADULT RUBY**, **WALTER** *and* **GRACE**. *When they return, it is the next morning, and* **WALTER** *is in his orchard, picking apples from an unseen tree. After a second,* **SID** *appears; he watches* **WALTER** *for a few seconds without speaking.)*

SID. Mr. Zweifel…

*(***WALTER** *looks up at* **SID.***)*

Picking fruit, huh? Apples, right?

*(***WALTER** *doesn't respond, instead resumes his chore.)*

Mr. Zweifel, I'm Sid Lazansky. Frieda told you about me last night. I thought I should, you know, come by and…apologize.

(silence)

Mr. Zweifel, are you listening to me, sir? I'm not a drinker. But the beer was my idea. It won't happen again – I promise.

(beat)

Mr. Zweifel, I wish you'd look at me, sir.

*(***WALTER** *doesn't.)*

I'm twenty-four…Frieda's younger, of course, but we've taken to each other and my parents…well they think she's a special young lady. So, in a couple of years, who knows…?

(beat)

Frieda said you and Mrs. Zweifel were twenty when you got married. Is that right?

*(***WALTER** *continues to ignore* **SID** *who makes one more effort.)*

I'm deferred, Mr. Zweifel. A heart murmur, you know? Rheumatic fever when I was nine. I tried to enlist – army, navy both, as a matter of fact. And I'm Jewish. Nothing I can do about that – being Jewish, I mean. And honestly, sir, I wouldn't do anything about it if I could. I'm proud of who I am.

(WALTER continues to ignore SID.)

I think I know why Frieda didn't want me to meet you –

WALTER. *(looks up at the unseen tree)* Should I cut it down?

SID. I didn't hear you, Mr. Zwiefel.

WALTER. This apple tree. Should I cut it down?

SID. I don't know much about fruit trees…

(also looks up at an unseen tree)

It looks healthy to me.

WALTER. The apples are green.

SID. Good green apples. Then I guess I don't understand why you'd want to – ?

WALTER. I prefer red.

SID. It's your tree, Mr. Zweifel –

WALTER. Most people prefer red.

(SID takes a long look at WALTER before speaking.)

SID. You're trying to tell me something, aren't you, Mr. Zweifel?

WALTER. *(looks up at SID, sadly)* Shame – it's a good-looking tree…

SID. I'm a green apple. Is that it?

WALTER. You leave it standing, you curse the apple.

SID. Good bye, Mr. Zweifel…

WALTER. You cut it down, you…you curse yourself.

(SID turns to exit.)

The rest of your life…you curse yourself.

(WALTER has begun to breathe heavily; SID notices.)

SID. Mr. Zweifel, are you okay?

(WALTER takes several deep breaths as SID approaches him, then takes a seat on an upside down bucket; SID bends to one knee along side.)

Is it your heart, Mr. Zweifel?

(SID looks at WALTER more closely. It's obvious he's crying.)

Mr. Zweifel…

(SID tries to put his hands on WALTER's shoulders, but WALTER pushes them away.)

WALTER. *Go!*

(SID hesitates.)

Go on! Leave me be!

(SID stands, then steps slowly away from WALTER who remains huddled in tears. SID looks up at WALTER's green apple tree, then exits. Only WALTER remains as the lights come up on ADULT RUBY.)

ADULT RUBY. When Pop didn't show up for supper late that afternoon, Mama went looking for him in his orchard. What she found was a wounded man – not physically – but emotionally. When she told me he had cried in front of her and apparently in front of Sid as well, I reacted strangely. For the first time I felt compassion for the man who had given me life, but whose soul I had never really known. I knew what Frieda's reaction would be, so I waited up for her...

(Lights down on ADULT RUBY and WALTER, up on YOUNG RUBY who sits on the steps of the porch. After a few seconds, FRIEDA appears; she carries a small suitcase and attempts to step past YOUNG RUBY.)

YOUNG RUBY. Hey, stop!

FRIEDA. Get out of my way, Ruby!

(YOUNG RUBY grabs FRIEDA's arm.)

YOUNG RUBY. I know what happened, sort of...with Pop and Sid this morning. I'd be furious too. So I've decided...I'm going with you.

FRIEDA. *What are you talking about?*

YOUNG RUBY. You're moving out, aren't you? Well, I'm going with you.

FRIEDA. Get out of my way, Ruby!

(Again, FRIEDA tries to step by RUBY; again RUBY stops her.)

YOUNG RUBY. Where are we staying?

FRIEDA. *Stop it, Ruby!*

YOUNG RUBY. With Mr. and Mrs. Lazansky maybe?

FRIEDA. I don't know where I'm staying, okay?

YOUNG RUBY. Shouldn't we know before we leave – ?

FRIEDA. Have you lost your marbles, Ruby?

YOUNG RUBY. Have you, Frieda?

(silence)

Pop cried. When he talked to Sid. Did Sid tell you?

FRIEDA. Of course he did!

YOUNG RUBY. Whatdaya think that means?

FRIEDA. Nothing! It doesn't mean anything!

YOUNG RUBY. I think it means he's sorry…for a lot of things we don't understand. But then, what do I know?

FRIEDA. He should be sorry. He hates Poles. Hates Jews…

YOUNG RUBY. Does he?

*(**FRIEDA** and **RUBY** look at one another as the lights dim to black.)*

*(Lights up on **HELGA** and **GRACE**. It is early the following morning. **GRACE** enters, looks out a window. After a moment, **HELGA** enters)*

HELGA. You're lucky this morning, Mama. It's my turn to fix breakfast.

GRACE. Uh-huh.

HELGA. I make a good fried egg I hear.

GRACE. Who's that walking up the road?

*(**HELGA** joins **GRACE** at the window.)*

HELGA. Rose, I think.

GRACE. That's strange – it's so early.

HELGA. You ask me, Rose does a lot of strange things these days.

GRACE. What's in her hand?

HELGA. I can't tell from here, Mama.

GRACE. What does it look like?

HELGA. I don't know.

GRACE. It's a piece of paper I think.

HELGA. You can ask her in a minute.

*(**GRACE** steps to a chair and sits. A few anxious seconds later, **ROSE** enters.)*

GRACE. Why are you walking so early, Rose?

HELGA. Mama's wants to know what you've got in your hand. Looks to me like a piece of paper, Mama.

GRACE. Honey, what's in your hand?

(silence)

HELGA. Mama asked you a question, Rose.

(silence)

GRACE. *(fearful it's bad news about Stan)* No, Rose…no.

HELGA. It's not a telegram, Mama. That's not a telegram, is it, Rose?

*(**GRACE** crosses to **ROSE**.)*

ROSE. *No, Mama!*

GRACE. What is it, Rose?

ROSE. Mama, sit down! I don't know what it is.

HELGA. I can see – it's just a piece of paper.

ROSE. *I don't know what it says!*

HELGA. What are you saying, Rose? Mama, what is she saying?

GRACE. Be quiet, Helga!

ROSE. It's a letter. In Polish. It's from somebody in Stan's unit I think. It was mailed from a hospital. I had it translated. I haven't read it…

GRACE. It's good news! If it's from a hospital – it's good news, Rose. Don't you think it's good news, Helga?

*(**ROSE** stands and walks to a back door. **GRACE** rises and makes an effort to join her.)*

ROSE. NOBODY!

(GRACE stops. She and HELGA watch as ROSE exits. Uneasy, they sit in silence for an extended period. Abruptly, the stillness is broken by a long, wrenching, mournful WAIL. Lights up on ADULT RUBY.)

ADULT RUBY. I was in my room – snug in the only safe place I still had – when I heard it.

(GRACE and HELGA rise and rush to ROSE's room.)

Nothing will equal the horror I felt as Rose's lament resounded through my room, into every bone in my body. I covered my head – as if a pillow would protect me…us…from the terrible sadness, the awful ramifications I expected to follow.

(It's that evening, and a floor lamp is on in the parlor. HELGA is in the room.)

It was evening before Mama managed to get the letter from Rose.

(GRACE enters the parlor. She carries the translation.)

Only then did we know Rose's terrible news. Stan – the translation said – had been a gallant soldier who had served his unit with distinction to the end. According to the writer, the end was not that Stan had died in combat, but that he was missing in action…and presumed dead.

(HELGA takes the translation, reads it, then passes it to WALTER who also reads it. All are devastated, particularly GRACE who weeps openly. After a moment, WALTER exits.)

HELGA. Missing doesn't have to mean he's…It's not like it's a telegram, Mama. Maybe he's with another unit… maybe he's been captured.

(Lights begin to dim to black.)

Mama, missing doesn't mean he's…

(Lights dim to black on all. In the darkness, we hear GRACE's sobs.)

(Later that evening. Lights up on **ROSE** *who sits on the steps of the porch. We hear a car door slam; she looks in that direction.)*

ROSE. Stan? Is that you?

FRIEDA. *(She comes into view.)* It's me, Rose. Did you mean to call me, Stan?

ROSE. I thought you might be him.

FRIEDA. What are you talking about, Rose?

ROSE. He'll be along soon you know.

FRIEDA. Stan is in –

ROSE. I know perfectly well where he is.

FRIEDA. Where do you think he is?

ROSE. In France, of course. But he'll be along soon.

*(***FRIEDA***, shaken by the encounter, enters the parlor.* **ROSE** *remains seated on a porch step. As* **ROSE** *speaks, she rocks back and forth.)*

I know you're out there.

(beat)

Stan, do you hear me? I know you're out there – somewhere you're out there.

(remembers something)

I'll put on my blue dress – that's what I'll do. Remember? I wore it the first night we went out. You told me I looked like a Polish princess. I waited then too. I thought you weren't coming, but you did. You said I looked like a princess. I'll put it on – then you'll come.

(hears something in the darkness, stops rocking, looks out)

Stan, is that you?

*(***WALTER** *appears from the darkness. He's been listening.)*

I had hoped you were Stan.

WALTER. Come inside, Rose.

ROSE. You haven't seen him, have you?

WALTER. Rose, please –

ROSE. Maybe he saw you. He thinks you don't like him. You don't, do you?

WALTER. Oh, Rose –

ROSE. Go inside now! So he can come!

> (**WALTER** *doesn't know what to say.*)
>
> *Go inside!*
>
> (*thinks of something important*)
>
> I'll put on my blue dress – that's what I'll do.
>
> (**GRACE** *appears in the doorway.*)
>
> *Yes!* I'll put on my blue dress. I'll look like a princess. Then he'll come.

GRACE. Rose, please come in.

> (**GRACE** *steps to* **ROSE**, *takes* **ROSE**'s *arm;* **ROSE** *resists.*)
>
> I need help, Walter.

ROSE. (*backing away from* **WALTER**) Don't touch me! Don't come near me! *Don't ever come near me!*

GRACE. Rose –

ROSE. (*pointing his finger at* **WALTER**) I know what he did!

GRACE. *He's your father.*

ROSE. I KNOW WHAT HE DID!

> (**GRACE** *slaps* **ROSE**. *The blow sounds like a GUNSHOT.*)
>
> *That sound!*
>
> (*beat, looking in various directions*)
>
> *What was that sound?*
>
> (*listening more intently now*)
>
> Something's banging! Listen! Louder! Louder! Bang! Bang! It's closer! Much closer now!
>
> (*looking intently now*)
>
> Smoke…everywhere smoke…noise…*that terrible noise!*
>
> (*after a second, appears to see someone*)

STAN IS THAT YOU?

(hysterical now)

RUN, STAN! RUN. NO. NO. *Not that way. This way...* THIS WAY. BANG! *Please, Stan...run to me.* BANG!

(looking in the opposite direction now, a sense of real panic)

Don't shoot him! *Don't shoot him.* DON'T...SHOOT HIM...*DON'T...*

*(**ROSE** slumps to the porch. The sound of her knees hitting the decking produces a BANG that resembles a gunshot. **GRACE** holds **ROSE**, and they rock back and forth as the lights on them begin to dim. Lights up on **ADULT RUBY**.)*

ADULT RUBY. Mama was able to get Rose to a bedroom where she remained for the better part of a week. For the rest of us, especially Mama and Pop, it was as if the darkest cloud in the universe had descended upon us, wrapping us in perpetual state of despair. Mama, of course, continued to worry about Frieda and her relationship with Sid, but it was Rose – her hostility toward Pop, her increasing delusions...the fear of what she might do next – that served as a ticking bomb for all of us.

*(Later that evening. Lights dim on **ADULT RUBY**. We hear the sound of crickets – they sound very much a ticking clock – as the lights come back up on **YOUNG RUBY** and **WALTER**. They sit together on a porch step. **RUBY** looks up to the evening sky.)*

YOUNG RUBY. Star light, star bright, first star I see tonight... I wish I may, I wish I might...

(She pretends she's unable to remember the rest.)

Help me, Pop.

*(**WALTER** doesn't respond.)*

Pop, did you hear me – ?

WALTER. I wish I may, I wish I might...*have the wish, I wish tonight.*

YOUNG RUBY. Have the wish, I wish tonight...

(Another silence during which it's obvious **YOUNG RUBY** *makes a wish.)*

Don't you want to know what I wished for?

*(***WALTER** *remains in his own world.)*

Maybe I wished I was in New York City...Rebecca Ruby is in the studios of the Columbia Broadcasting System...telling the world this awful war is over. That would've been a good wish, wouldn't it, Pop?

*(***WALTER** *manages to nod.)*

Except I wished for something else ... something about you.

(Silence as **WALTER** *and* **YOUNG RUBY***'s eyes lock on one another.)*

YOUNG RUBY. Don't you want to know what it was?

*(***WALTER** *looks at* **RUBY***; he wants to hear)*

I wished I knew a lot of things. Things like...like why you don't dance with Mama anymore.

*(***RUBY** *looks at* **WALTER**, *pleading for a response. He looks away.)*

Pop, I'm trying to understand...I need help ...

*(***RUBY** *looks to* **WALTER** *for answers; there aren't any; after a second, she smiles, then looks up.)*

I wish I may, I wish I might...have the wish, I wish tonight...

*(***YOUNG RUBY** *rises, steps to* **WALTER**, *giving him a big hug which he returns in a lesser fashion. She exits. Seconds later* **GRACE** *approaches* **WALTER** *who still sits on the porch step. We hear the sounds of crickets; more than ever, they sound like a ticking clock.)*

GRACE. I surprised myself this morning, Walter. I woke up smiling almost…thinking how – before this awful war started – how you couldn't walk into this house without hearing little girls laughing.

(smiling, remembering fondly)

I played a game with them – I don't think you knew that. I'd ask each of them to describe the boy they wanted to marry. Helga – years before Jimmy showed up – talked about walking down the aisle with whoever asked her first. Frieda – full of herself even then – wanted to marry a rich college boy, live as far from us as she possible – China was too close. Ruby – bless her heart – always told me the same thing. Come hell or high water, she was going to New York City where some big-time radio man would be waiting with open arms and a wedding ring. And Rose…?

(beat)

Rose told me she wanted to find somebody just like her daddy.

*(**ROSE** enters; she's heard **GRACE**'s speech. She's disheveled.)*

ROSE. He all but had me wrapped around his little finger, didn't he, Mama?

GRACE. I didn't see you there, Rose.

ROSE. Oh, we were something, Pop.

GRACE. Pretty fall mornings, the two of you'd go into the orchard – oh, sweetie, you were always his favorite… you'd pick fruit for hours –

ROSE. He'd hold the basket, I'd fill it up. I'd eat the biggest one. Juice would run down my chin…he'd wipe it off, give me a little kiss on the cheek. Remember, Pop?

(silence, except for the incessant chirping)

GRACE. Of course, he remembers, Rose. Walter, tell her you remember. Honey, he'd brag how good you were at picking out the ripe ones.

ROSE. I loved being there with you, Pop.

GRACE. Listen to what Rose is telling you, Walter.

ROSE. Those were the good old days.

GRACE. I'm so happy you're feeling better.

ROSE. What happened to them, Pop?

GRACE. *(understanding things really haven't changed)* Walk a while with me, Rose –

ROSE. *I asked you a question, Pop?*

GRACE. It's such a pretty night –

(silence, except for the sound of the crickets)

ROSE. Pop, I'm waiting.

WALTER. *(after a second, with great pain)* Rose, I'm sorry.

ROSE. He's sorry, Mama.

GRACE. Yes! And that's a start.

ROSE. Ask him what he's sorry about.

GRACE. He's sorry about Stan – aren't you, Walter?

ROSE. Sorry he's dead?

GRACE. He's missing, Rose.

ROSE. Sorry he killed him?

GRACE. I will not listen to this, Rose.

ROSE. Is that what you're sorry about, Pop?

GRACE. No more –

ROSE. I have to know why he's sorry.

GRACE. Rose, I beg you.

ROSE. Sorry about the way you treated him? Sorry you made him grovel like an animal, made him defend himself…where he came from…what he believed? Is that what you're sorry about?

WALTER. *(continuing to look away)* Yes.

ROSE. Sorry you fed him Nazi hate? Hitler, the savior of Europe. So what if he destroyed Poland in the process? Sorry about that too, Pop?

WALTER. Yes!

*(**WALTER** appears to be having difficulty breathing.)*

ROSE. Sorry you told me he wasn't good enough for me?
GRACE. Oh, Walter.
ROSE. I said, "Pop, I love Stan." He stopped talking to me. Did you hate him that much? Or were you punishing me because I brought somebody home – planned to marry someone you didn't approve of?

*(Silence as **WALTER** looks away.)*

Oh, so many questions, so few answers.

GRACE. *(sensing **WALTER**'s breathing difficulties)* Is it your heart again, Walter?
ROSE. Before you die, Pop –
GRACE. How awful, Rose!
ROSE. *Before he dies –*
GRACE. Walter, sit down please.

*(**WALTER** remains standing, his breathing problems continue; **GRACE** is terrified at what is happening before her.)*

ROSE. I need an answer –
GRACE. Can't you see what you're doing to him, Rose?
ROSE. Why, Pop? When he told me he loved me, when we were almost married? Why…all of a sudden…did he leave? If he loved me, why – ?
GRACE. Of course, he loved you, Rose.
ROSE. *How do you know, Mama?*
GRACE. You could see it, Rose. The way the boy looked at you.
ROSE. I told myself…I would know – all the awful doubt would be gone…everybody would know! – when the war was over…when Stan came back. *Mama…he can't come back.*
GRACE. Oh, he loved you, honey. With all of his heart, the boy loved you –
ROSE. HOW DO YOU KNOW?

(silence, except for the crickets)

It's up to you, Stan. Tell me…let me know…did you love me?

(more desperately)

I'm not hearing anything. Stan, I need an answer. If you loved me, tell me –

WALTER. *Yes!*

(turns slowly to face **ROSE***)*

Yes! He loved you, Rose!

ROSE. Someone who knows all about hate is talking about love.

WALTER. He told me!

ROSE. Can you hear him, Stan? The person who despised you –

GRACE. No more, Rose!

ROSE. A Pole is like an apple with a rotten spot. Quick… toss it…get it out of here…before it spoils the good ones. Wasn't that it, Pop? Out with the coal-mining Polack – don't let him spoil the German. *Wasn't that it, Pop?*

(Silence, except for the crickets that seem louder now.)

WALTER. I didn't hate him, Rose –

ROSE. Lies now…

WALTER. I respected him –

ROSE. He hears you, Pop.

WALTER. His loyalty. He had two loves. You, Rose, and Poland.

GRACE. You know that's true, Rose. Remember how proud he was of his was country?

WALTER. That's all I needed to know…to get him to do what I…thought was best for you.

ROSE. Stories now….

WALTER. Not because I hated him…because I loved you.

ROSE. Oh, do you hear the stories, Stan?

WALTER. I kept after him. Kept reminding him what Germany did to Poland. Horrible things – I knew they were horrible – but I used them. No choice, I told him. Poland needed him now. Win the war, revenge the killings, come back to Rose. Only a coward would refuse.

ROSE. He was no coward!

WALTER. He refused, because he didn't want to leave you! He loved you more than he loved his country.

GRACE. Do you hear, Rose?

ROSE. Words…empty words.

(WALTER hesitates. His discomfort is peaking.)

WALTER. A hundred times I've hated what I did next.

GRACE. We're listening, Pop.

WALTER. I don't know that I can tell you, Rose. I don't know that I have the words.

(A pause as he considers his words, bravely.)

Stan would go drinking at the Polish Lodge in Bluefield…with his friends – I knew that –

ROSE. Oh, he loved to tell stories…he was the life of the party…oh, how they'd laugh at his stories…

(We hear laughter and perhaps polka music.)

WALTER. His friends were there –

(Lights begin to dim on the parlor and come up in the Polish Lodge – again, created by lighting and sound. We hear more laughter and see STAN standing, a drink in one hand, a cigarette in the other; he laughs and speaks but we hear neither at first.)

WALTER. I watched him…drinking his vodka, laughing, speaking to them in Polish. I didn't understand what he was saying, but that didn't stop me.

STAN. *(Phonetic representation of Polish words; see addendum for English/Polish.)* Vence poviadam yemu tso vijowbim yego v rane.

(more laughter)

WALTER. *(in the dark, unseen)* Tell them you're a coward too.

(WALTER enters the beam of light; STAN is surprised.)

Tell them how you're going to kill Germans…win the war…make mother Poland proud.

STAN. *(speaking to his unseen friends)* This is Walter. Walter is Rose's father…

WALTER. Tell them how –

STAN. Go home, Walter! This is not your place here. Don't cause trouble, please.

WALTER. Do they understand English? Do you friends who live in America…do they understand – ?

(motioning to STAN's unseen friends)

STAN. Understand English, yes. Please go home. I beg you…

WALTER. *(now addressing STAN's friends)* Let me tell you why this man wants me to leave –

STAN. *(explaining something to his friends)* Nie svracia uvagien na tego chwovieka!

WALTER. He's a liar, that's why.

STAN. Walter, you have too much beer…go home.

WALTER. He swore he'd fight for his country…for Poland. Didn't you, Stanislaw Kulikowski?

STAN. I would join the Polish Free Forces…I told you that – yes.

WALTER. Still, here he stands, taking about the how Germans destroyed his country, killed his sister. You are all old men – like me – but he is young and here he is… drinking vodka, laughing…while your country –

STAN. *(explaining things to his unseen friends)* You see, I met beautiful Rose. I decide…

(There's laughter from his friends; STAN doesn't continue.)

WALTER. Go on, Stanislaw Kulikowski…tell them why you refused to fight for your country.

STAN. Because I love your daughter, Walter.

(more laughter)

WALTER. Honor your word!

STAN. *(again explaining to his friends, fearing they don't understand)* Rose and I are engaged…we are to get married, have a wonderful life…in America. This is my home, Walter. I love America.

WALTER. *Honor your word, Stanislaw Kulikowski.*

(silence)

They're waiting…

(Silence, as **STAN** *studies the faces of his unseen countrymen.)*

If you love Poland, Stanislaw Kulikowski…honor your word!

(Silence as **STAN** *continues to look at the unseen Poles; finally, pressured, he lifts his glass in a toast.)*

STAN. *Nieh duwugo shiye Polska!* Long live Poland!

MEN. *(Offstage)* NIEH DUWUGO SHIYE POLSKA!

(We hear applause from **STAN**'s *friends as the lights go down quickly to black, then come up on the parlor where* **GRACE**, **ROSE** *and* **WALTER**, *who has rejoined them, assume the positions they occupied previously.* **WALTER** *is a defeated man, fighting for breath and some semblance of forgiveness and self-respect.* **GRACE**, *in tears, attempts to comfort her daughter. Instead, it is* **ROSE** *who comforts her mother.)*

ROSE. Mama, don't cry. He loved me! I know that now. He would've come home! We would've had a wonderful life!

*(***ROSE** *– in her own world now – turns, steps to the porch.)*

It's true, isn't it, Stan? You loved me. You would've come home. We would've had a wonderful life.

(Sits on step, begins to rock back and forth, looking into the dark.)

I would've put on my blue dress – I wore it the first night, remember? You told me I looked like a princess…

(**GRACE**, *with great sadness, watches* **ROSE** *who is oblivious to everything around her. There's a long silence.*)

GRACE. Walter. Walter, I want you to look at me…

(**WALTER** *doesn't look at* **GRACE**.)

Tell me it isn't true, Walter. Tell me the man who stole my heart, gave me four beautiful daughters, held me when I was alone and scared…tell me that man wouldn't do something so awful. Walter, look at me… tell me you didn't do that to Rose.

(*Silence.* **WALTER** *looks at* **ROSE**. **GRACE** *thinks she had her answer.*)

God, Walter, no. Why…?

(*remembers the confession, rallying around that thought*)

You wanted her to marry somebody German, somebody like Jimmy, someone like you. You want her to be happy…that's what this is all about…

(*After a moment, shaking her head, unable or unwilling to buy the logic of that idea.*)

(**WALTER** *crosses slowly to* **ROSE** *who remains huddled on a step of the porch. He bends down, gives her long hug, then turns and walks into his unseen orchard.*)

(*to herself, quietly so* **ROSE** *doesn't hear*) He made it up. Oh, Walter, you made it up, didn't you? The whole story…meeting Stan in the bar. There was no meeting, was there, Walter? He left…Stan left, because he…

(*Looks at* **ROSE**, *doesn't continue her thought fearing* **ROSE** *might understand.*)

And you made it up. You gave Rose the answer she wanted…because you love her.

(*beat*)

It's our secret, Walter…

(**GRACE** *steps out onto the porch, sits next to* **ROSE**. *They rock back and forth together for a long moment.*)

Your daddy loves you. Remember, Rose…your daddy loves you.

(beat, then softly, pleadingly, hopefully)

You do love her, don't you, Walter?

*(Lights down on the porch, up on **ADULT RUBY** who stands with the photo album in her hand.)*

ADULT RUBY. He loved all of us I think. Maybe – if Mama was right – too much. Certainly in ways we never understood.

*(looking at **GRACE**, smiling)*

Mama kept her promise...she didn't say a word...

*(a beam of light comes up; **WALTER** steps into it.)*

Until five years later – after Pop, alone in his orchard – had died. By then...

*(**ROSE** steps into the same beam of light. She looks straight ahead, expressionless.)*

Rose had slipped into a make-believe world only she understood. In this house – too much of it alone – she'd live another forty years...never looking at another man, never dancing another dance. Yesterday, in a simple ceremony, we buried her.

*(**GRACE** joins **WALTER** and **ROSE** in the beam of light.)*

Mama, devastated by Rose's decline into dementia and Pop's sudden death – only two years before her own – shared with us, Pop's account of his exchange with Stan. We reacted to the story she told in very different ways.

*(**HELGA** joins **WALTER**, **ROSE** and **GRACE** in the beam.)*

Helga – who by then had two sons with Jimmy who returned as he had left – accepted what Mama wanted us to believe.

*(**FRIEDA** joins the circle.)*

Frieda, sadly – perhaps remembering Pop's treatment of Sid Lazansky who – by then was a memory himself – thought Pop, at best, had manipulated Stan, to get him to enlist...at worst, that he was as hate-filled as

Mr. Jennings and others claimed. Either way, someone incapable of scarifying himself for one of us.

(beat)

And Rebecca Ruby…?

(YOUNG RUBY *appears, completing the family circle.)*

In the person of Ruby Zweifel Frederick…the mother of four sons…she never went to New York. Never ruled the airwaves. And never knew what to believe.

(a long beat, looking over her shoulder into the parlor)

Back, now – for the last time – searching for answers… discovering – perhaps as a blessing – the uncertainty remains.

(For a long moment, she looks at the photo album, than closes it, doing so with a sense of closure. She gathers her thoughts before speaking bravely, emotionally.)

ADULT RUBY. So…I shall choose to recall the before…those special, joyous times…

(Fade in music from the opening scene. The volume is so low that we can't be sure we're hearing it.)

When youthful voices – giggling over simple pleasures – filled this space. When parents in love with each other…and with life…

(beat)

Danced the night away.

(If we look closely, we see the characters moving ever so slightly to the music…a gentle, almost indistinguishable sway. The music continues as the lights fade slowly to black.)

End of Play

PROPERTIES

Photo Album
Blue Star service flag (single blue star centered in a while rectangle bordered in red displayed in a window)
Magazine
Radio from the 40s
Paper and pen
Pan (to hold hot water)
Shade on window
Unshelled peas
Bowl to hold shelled peas
Afghan/light blanket
Table
Lamp
Letter
Envelope
Bible
Telegram (yellow paper)
Apples
Buckets
Suitcase
Cigarette
Bar drinks (beer, for example)

SOUND EFFECTS

Radio bulletins (multiple as scripted)
Music from the 1940s (multiple as specified)
Radio commercials from the 40s (optional)
Men's voices at the produce market
Slam of car door
Sound of car accelerating
Conductor's voice at station
Locomotive whistle
Ladies wail
Slap (sounds like a gunshot)
Bang (also sounds like a gunshot)
Sounds of crickets
A glass for liquor
Voices, polka music, laughter, applause of Stan's friends at a beer hall (as scripted)

POLISH-ENGLISH PRONUNCIATION GUIDE

Polish: *Wiec powladam jemu co widzialbym jego w ranie.*
*Phonetically: *Vence poviadam yemu tso vijowbim yego v rane.*
English Translation: So I told him I would see him in the morning.

Polish: *Nie zwraca uwage ne tego czlowieka.*
*Phonetically: *Nie svracia uragien na tego chwovieka.*
English Translation: Do not pay this man any attention.

Polish: *Niech dlugo zyje Polska!*
*Phonetically: *Nieh duwugo shiye Polska!*
English Translation: Long Live Poland!

Verbiage included in script.

Also by
Ron Osborne...

First Baptist of Ivy Gap

Showtime at First Baptist

Seeing Stars in Dixie

Wise Women

Please visit our website **samuelfrench.com** for complete descriptions and licensing information

www.ingramcontent.com/pod-product-compliance
Lightning Source LLC
Chambersburg PA
CBHW070648300426
44111CB00013B/2318